NUTSHELLS

CRIMINAL LAW IN A NUTSHELL

THIRD EDITION

by

Marianne Giles, LL.B., B.C.L. (OXON.)
Lecturer in Law,
University of Kent at Canterbury

London ● Sweet & Maxwell ● 1993

Published in 1993 by
Sweet & Maxwell Limited of
South Quay Plaza, 183 Marsh Wall, London E14 9FT
Typeset by
Wyvern Typesetting Ltd, Bristol
Printed in England by Clays Ltd,
St Ives plc

A CIP Catalogue record
for this book is available
from the British Library

ISBN 0-421-474408

CONTENTS

INTRODUCTION

This book is written solely as a revision text. Any introductory comments on the criminal law as a whole would therefore be out of place. I have instead concentrated on the main topics which can be found on the vast majority of criminal law syllabuses. Recommendations contained in the Draft Criminal Code, Law Commission Working Papers and Reports are incorporated where relevant.

When revising, the student should not try to cover every topic. He should pick the topics he knows best and in which he is most interested. A student doing otherwise could find himself spending half the examination time deciding which questions he can best answer and the other half answering them badly because he has not got enough time.

Conversely, of course, the student should not revise too few topics. He should be able to answer the correct number of questions and to have some choice. As in all legal subjects, the topics in criminal law are inter-related and there are some topics which no student should leave out of his revision programme. They can crop up in any problem question on any substantive topic and can be relevant in many essay questions too. I would class all the general principles under this head but most particularly *actus reus* and *mens rea*, and the defences. However well a student thinks he knows offences against the person and offences against property, he cannot do himself justice unless he is aware of the relevance of the general principles to them.

Marianne Giles.
September 1992.

1. ACTUS REUS

A person cannot ordinarily be found guilty of a serious criminal offence unless two elements are present: the *actus reus* or guilty act and the *mens rea* or guilty mind. A wrongful act on its own therefore cannot usually be criminal unless the wrongful state of mind required for that offence is also present.

WHAT IS AN ACTUS REUS?

An *actus reus* consists of more than just an act. It also consists of whatever circumstances and consequences are recognised for liability for the offence in question—in other words all the elements of an offence other than the mental element.

Some crimes require the production of consequences or results, such as murder and criminal damage. Others merely require a course of conduct, such as theft and rape.

If any element of the *actus reus* is missing then there is no liability.

Authority: *Deller* (1952). D had made what he thought was a false representation in order to sell his car. In fact the representation was true. He was charged under the Larceny Act 1916 with an offence of obtaining property by false pretences, (see now Theft Act 1968, s.15). One part of the *actus reus*, the circumstance that the representation he made was false, was missing. Therefore there was no liability. The fact that this was purely accidental was irrelevant.

THE ACCUSED'S CONDUCT MUST BE VOLUNTARY

The accused's conduct must be "voluntary" if he is to incur liability. It may be involuntary for a variety of reasons.

Automatism

This is considered in more detail as a defence in Chapter 6. Automatism occurs when D performs a physical act or acts but is unaware of what he is doing, or is not in control of his actions.

Judges have defined automatism in various ways including "acts performed involuntarily," "unconscious involuntary action," and "involuntary movement of the . . . limbs of a person."

Automatism can be seen as relevant to *actus reus* in that the act is not a voluntary act, or alternatively in terms of *mens rea* in that there is no mental element present in relation to the act because the defendant is not aware of what (s)he is doing.

Physical force

The conduct may be involuntary in that it is physically forced by someone else, in which case there will be no *actus reus*.

Reflex actions

Sometimes people can respond to something with a spontaneous reflex action over which they have no control. Although slightly different, this is sometimes classed as a form of automatism. The classic example is that given in *Hill* v. *Baxter* (1958) of someone being stung by a swarm of bees while driving, and losing control of the car.

"STATE OF AFFAIRS" CASES

One group of cases which cannot be discussed in terms of voluntary acts are often referred to as the "state of affairs" cases. These are cases where the *actus reus* consists of circumstances and sometimes consequences but no "acts," *i.e.* "being" rather than "doing" offences.

Authority: *Larsonneur* (1933). D's conviction for an offence of "being an alien to whom leave to land in the United Kingdom has been refused" was upheld by the Court of Criminal Appeal. D was an alien, but she had been forcibly brought into the country by the Irish police. The *actus reus* of the crime consisted of the circumstances of being an alien, over which she had no control, and the circumstances of being in the U.K. over which she had no control either in these particular circumstances.

It is generally thought that D should have been allowed the "physical force" defence discussed above, but a more recent case may cast doubt upon this.

Authority: *Winzar* v. *Chief Constable of Kent* (1983). D was charged with "being found drunk in a highway contrary to section 12 of the Licensing Act 1872." D had been taken involuntarily to the highway by the police who had found him drunk in a hospital. In this case, too, one element of the *actus reus*, that of being in the highway, could be said to have occurred involuntarily, but as it was not an act but a state of affairs or a circumstance, this argument was not used and D's conviction was upheld.

These cases incidentally present problems of *mens rea* too. What was the guilty state of mind of Larsonneur or of Winzar? (See Chap. 2.)

CAUSATION

Questions of causation can present problems in the consideration of *actus reus*. In "result crimes" (*i.e.* where a consequence is part of the *actus reus*), not only must the prosecution prove a forbidden act in forbidden circumstances, but they must also prove that the defendant's conduct caused the required consequence.

This causal connection is often difficult to make. Murder is the major example of a result crime, (*i.e.* one where a consequence or consequences are part of the *actus reus*) and the problems can be illustrated in that context. There are four main problem areas:

(i) When is the act a substantial cause of death?
(ii) Cumulative and alternative causes.
(iii) What is the legal effect of an intervening event?
(iv) What is the legal effect of negligent medical treatment?

Substantial cause of death

For liability, D's conduct need not be the sole cause of death, but it must be a substantial cause. However this is impossible to quantify precisely. In many of the cases policy reasons, although not overtly expressed, obviously influence the courts in their decisions.

Authority: *obiter dicta* statements in *Dyson* (1908). The defendant's conviction was set aside on appeal because of a misdirection on another point, but the court said that if D had accelerated his victim's death within a year it was irrelevant that the victim had meningitis and would have died before long anyway.

Authority: *Adams* (1957). Devlin J. directed the jury that deliberately giving pain-killing drugs to shorten life could constitute murder even if the patient would die in a few weeks or months anyway. He went on to say that if drugs are given to relieve pain, and an incidental consequence is the shortening of life, then there is no liability. This is not an easy distinction to make. It seems to be a policy distinction which cannot be justified in strict logic, especially as motive is deemed to be irrelevant in criminal law.

Cumulative or alternative causes

It is much easier to establish liability if the defendant's act was one of a number of causes which together could be said to have caused the harm, than if it is merely one possible alternative cause.

Authority: *Watson* (1989). The victim was elderly and frail. Following a burglary, visits by police, and council repairmen, he suffered a heart attack and died. Although the defendants' convictions were quashed on appeal because the jury had not been properly directed on causation, it was clear that the burglary caused the visits by police and repair men which in turn might have caused the heart attack. This could establish a causal link. This situation is different from that where there are possible alternative causes. In such a case causation is more difficult to establish.

Authority: *Armstrong* (1989). The defendant supplied heroin and a syringe to a person who took the drug and subsequently died. Evidence showed that he had already consumed an amount of alcohol which could be fatal in itself. It was held that there was not sufficient evidence to establish whether it was only one of the possible causes or a combination of both which caused death.

Intervening events

Sometimes, after the defendant's initial act, there is an intervening act or event before the required consequence occurs which contributes to that consequence.

If the intervening act or event is completely unconnected with the defendant's act, was unforseeable, and would have brought about the consequence on its own, then he incurs no liability for homicide.

If the consequence is caused by a combination of the two causes, and the defendant's act remains a substantial cause, then the defendant will still be liable.

Authority: *Malcherek* (1981). D's victim was put on a life support machine as a result of the injuries he inflicted. After several days the machine was switched off and the victim died. D was convicted of murder and appealed on the issue of causation, which he said should have been put to the jury. The appeal was dismissed. The court said that D's act was a substantial cause of death and any other contributory cause was immaterial.

If the intervening act is an act of the victim himself then the courts ask whether the victim's response was "within a range of responses which might be anticipated." If so it will not break the chain of causation.

Authority: *Williams* (1991). D and another had picked up a hitch-hiker, and had threatened him with injury if he did not hand over his money. The issue of causation and a victim's response to threats arose because he subsequently fell out of the car as it was moving, and was killed. On appeal it was held that the jury should have been directed in the terms stated above on the question of the victim's intervening acts.

If on the other hand it is completely unforseeable then it can break the chain.

Authority: *Pagett* (1983). D was being pursued by armed policemen. In trying to escape he held a girl in front of him as protection and shot at the policemen. They instinctively fired back and the girl was killed. The court held that D's act had caused the death as the intervening act had been a forseeable consequence of his action and had not broken the chain of causation.

If the intervening act is a characteristic of the victim then it does not have to be foreseeable and will not break the chain of the causation. The thin skull rule will apply. The defendant's act must of course still be a substantial cause of the result. The widest interpretation of a victim's characteristic interprets religious convictions which result in certain acts or omissions as a characteristic which therefore does not have to be forseeable.

Authority: *Blaue* (1975). D stabbed his victim and pierced her lung. She required an immediate blood transfusion to save her life but she refused to have one on religious grounds. She subsequently died. The court held that a defendant must take his victim as he finds him, and the fact that the victim's reaction here was unforeseeable and arguably unreasonable was irrelevant.

Negligent medical treatment

A final set of cases where causation problems arise are those concerning negligent medical treatment of the original injury in homicide cases.

This is another area where policy considerations have influenced the courts and attitudes have changed over the years. The courts are now very unwilling as a matter of policy to lay blame on medical staff for deaths when there has been an initial unlawful act by someone else.

The two main cases in this area conflict with each other but the later case more accurately represents the law. The earlier case has subsequently been distinguished on its own particular facts and has very little general application any longer.

Authority: *Jordan* (1956). D had stabbed his victim who had died several days later after undergoing medical treatment. It was finally established on appeal that the wound had been healing well but the medical treatment was grossly negligent. The victim had been given an antibiotic to which he was allergic and large amounts of intravenous liquid. The court held that a jury might have reached a verdict of not guilty had they had all the medical evidence and expert opinion, and the conviction was quashed.

Authority: *Smith* (1959). D, a soldier had stabbed his victim, another soldier, who was carried to the medical officer in charge. The medical officer was dealing with a series of emergencies and failed to appreciate the seriousness of the victim's wounds. The treatment he gave him was not beneficial and may well have made his condition worse. The victim died. D was found guilty of murder and appealed. The court held that D's stabbing was an "operating and substantial cause" of death and the medical treatment was irrelevant. They distinguished *Jordan* on its particular facts and said that in that case the wound was merely the setting for the main and substantial cause of death, the medical treatment.

The Court of Appeal has recently confirmed the approach taken in *Smith*, indicating that *Jordan* has virtually no relevance any more, except in the most "extraordinary or extreme" case.

Authority: *Cheshire* (1991). D had caused the original wounds which had necessitated hospitalisation. The victim had contracted a respiratory infection which had resulted in a respiratory blockage. Although unusual, the doctors should have reacted more quickly. They failed to realise the seriousness of the blockage, and evidence showed that they were negligent in this respect. If the blockage had been treated properly it was very unlikely that death would have occurred. Nevertheless, despite the negligence, the Court held that D's act was an operating and substantial cause of death.

OMISSIONS

"Unless a statute specifically so provides, or . . . the common law imposes a duty upon one person to act in a particular way towards another . . . a *mere* omission to act [cannot lead to criminal liability]." (*Miller*, (1982).)

A positive duty to act exists in the following circumstances:

Special relationship

Where there is a special relationship between the defendant and the victim this can create a duty. The most obvious example is parent and child, but this is not the only one. Other examples occur where people are in positions of authority or responsibility.

Authority: *Gibbins and Proctor* (1918). The first defendant was the father of a child, and together with the second, female, defendant with whom he was living they omitted to feed the child so that it died. He was found liable. Their convictions for murder were upheld.

The relationship of doctor-patient can cause particular difficulties where the patient is a severely handicapped neo-nate. Although there is no separate rule within criminal law which exculpates doctors who do not treat these patients, it is clear that the extent of a doctor's duty in such a case is a very complex issue, and that the use of medication or extraordinary medical treatment may not be compulsory. This issue has been considered more recently in civil cases, in the context of duties toward a ward of court, for example.

Authority: *Re J.* (1991). This case concerned possible treatment to a severely mentally and physically handicapped five month old baby who intermittently needed to be put on a respirator in order to be kept alive. A High Court order was made (he was a ward of court) that should it become necessary again to use a machine to keep him breathing, it was up to doctors to decide whether that was the appropriate treatment. The implication is that there is no automatic duty to keep him alive at all costs.

Voluntary assumption of responsibility

If someone voluntarily assumes responsibility for another person then they also assume the positive duty to act for the general welfare of that person and may be liable for omissions which prove fatal.

Authority: *Gibbins and Proctor* (above). The female defendant, although not the mother of the child, had assumed responsibility by living with the father and the child.

Authority: *Stone and Dobinson* (1977). A couple had assumed voluntary responsibility for an aunt living with them. They omitted to care for her properly and did not realise that she needed medical attention. She died, and they were held liable for manslaughter.

Duty under a contract

A person may be under a positive duty to act because of his obligations under a contract. The duty may be to the other contracting party or to a third person.

Authority: *Pittwood* (1902). D was the keeper at a railway crossing who forgot to shut the gate before a train came. Someone crossing the line was struck by the train and killed. The court held that D owed a duty to all users of the crossing and not just to his employers. D was accordingly guilty of manslaughter.

Statutory duty

In some circumstances statute makes it a criminal offence to omit to do something. For example, section 170 of the Road Traffic Act 1988 makes it an offence, if one is involved in an accident, to omit to either report it within 24 hours to the police or to give all relevant details to any other person at the scene of the accident reasonably requesting them.

Duty due to defendant's prior conduct

If the defendant has acted positively although innocently to create a state of affairs which might cause damage or injury, and subsequently becomes aware of the danger he has created, there arises a duty to act reasonably to avert that danger.

Authority: *Miller* (1983). D was squatting in a house and fell asleep smoking. The mattress caught fire and he woke up. Instead of putting out the fire he moved into another room and went back to sleep. The house caught fire and the House of Lords held him liable for arson. D had unwittingly brought about a situation of danger to property. Once he realised this he was under a self-induced duty to act positively to avert it.

This final category of liability is a fairly recent one and there may be more to come.

Proposals for reform

The Law Commission has published a Consultation Paper (No. 122, 1992), on Offences Against the Person and General Principles. In it, the Commission makes the following recommendations relevant to this chapter.

1. Under clause 3 of the Draft Bill liability arises for failing to carry out a common law duty to act resulting in the commission of one of a series of specified offences, (intentional serious injury, torture, unlawful detention, kidnapping, abduction and aggravated abduction).

2. Under clause 24, the principle of supervening fault is incorporated as a general principle to cover the *Miller* situation. D will be liable if he does an act which caused or is causing a

result, and when he becomes aware of this he fails to take reasonable steps to stop or avert it.

SUMMARY

The main topics for revision are:

What is *Actus reus*?
(*Deller*)

Actus reus must be voluntary
Automatism (*H.M. Advocate* v. *Ritchie*)
Physical Force
Reflex Actions
Duress by Threats

"State of affairs" cases
"Being" crimes (*Larsonneur, Winzar* v. *Chief Constable of Kent*)

Causation
Substantial Cause (*Dyson, Adams*)
Cumulative or alternative causes (*Watson, Armstrong*)
Intervening Events (*Malcherek, Williams, Pagett, Blaue*)
Negligent Medical Treatment (*Jordan, Smith, Cheshire*)

Omissions
Special Relationship (*Gibbons and Proctor, Re J.*)
Assumption of Responsibility (*Gibbons and Proctor, Stone and Dobinson*)
Duty under Contract (*Pittwood*)
Statutory Duty
Duty due to Defendant's Prior Conduct (*Miller*)

Reforms
Law commission working paper.

---

2. MENS REA

Mens rea is the culpable state of mind which is necessary, together with the *actus reus*, for a criminal offence to be committed. *Mens rea*, where needed, can vary from crime to crime, but there are four states of mind which separately or together can constitute the necessary *mens rea* for a criminal offence.   ✔

Shop.

INTENTION

Intention must first be distinguished from motive, which is irrelevant to liability.

Authority: *Steane* (1947). The principle that motive is irrelevant is very well established in the criminal law, and the case of *Steane* does not openly dispute it. The court talks in terms of intention, and the decision is explained in terms of intention, but many commentators see it as an example of a case where motive was *not* irrelevant. The student must make up his own mind. In *Steane*, D was charged with broadcasting "with intent to assist the enemy." He had broadcast for the enemy during World War II because of threats to his family. The court held that he was not guilty because his intent was not to assist the enemy, but to save his family. The student should consider this in the light of the definition of intent in terms of direct and oblique intent. One possible explanation may be that this was a very unusual case where only direct intent, *i.e.* desiring the consequence, was sufficient for *mens rea*.

Direct and oblique intent

Intention in law has a slightly different meaning than in ordinary everyday language. In law intent was said to consist of direct intent, where the consequence is desired, and oblique intent where it is not. The defendant is said to have an oblique intent where he sees the consequence as certain or virtually certain, and although he does not positively desire it (he may in fact hope it does not happen), he goes ahead with his actions anyway. Although the former is still intention as a matter of law, the courts have, in recent cases, treated the latter simply as being capable as a question of fact of constituting evidence of intention. The matter is therefore left to the jury.

In the past it has been difficult to draw the line between intention and recklessness. Oblique intent has been defined in terms of foresight of likelihood or high probability, rather than of certainty, and the difference between intention and recklessness therefore depended solely on how likely the defendant thought the consequence to be. It was simply a question of degree.

Where did recklessness end and intent begin? It was not clear, even to the House of Lords. The recent case law has failed to lay down a clear definition of intention as a matter of law. It has simply been made clear that desire of consequences IS intent as a matter of law, and lack of foresight of consequences IS NOT intent as a matter of law. The grey area in between, covering foresight of consequences, is left as a question of fact for the jury to decide, albeit with strong guidance from a judge.

Authority: *Moloney* (1985). D and his stepfather had been having a discussion about firearms, and had a shooting contest to see who could load and fire a shotgun faster. D won but his stepfather had challenged him to fire a live bullet. D did this and killed his stepfather. He was charged with murder.

The direction to the jury on intention was in terms of foresight of probability following *Hyam* v. *D.P.P.* (1974): *i.e.* D had the necessary *mens rea* for murder if he foresaw death as a probable consequence of his actions, even if he did not desire it. The case went on appeal to the House of Lords on the question of whether foresight of probability of death or really serious injury could be sufficient *mens rea* for murder. The House of Lords held that it could not. Only the *intent* to kill or cause really serious injury would be enough.

Foresight of high probability is not automatically equivalent to intention. It becomes a question for the jury to decide whether foresight of high probability, or foresight of the "natural consequences" as Lord Bridge put it, is an indication of intent.

Authority: *Hancock* (1986). D and another had thrown items down on to a motorway from a bridge in order to block the road and stop a taxi carrying a working miner during the miners' strike. A concrete block hit the windscreen of the taxi and the driver was killed. On the question of intent the House of Lords said that Lord Bridge's statements in *Moloney* regarding foresight of natural consequences could be confusing if used to direct a jury without more explanation. Natural consequences were not the same as probable consequences. A jury should be told that the greater the probability of a consequence occurring, the more likely that it was foreseen, and the more likely it is that it was foreseen, the more likely it is that it was intended. *But that is all*. Any such inference regarding intention was to be made by the jury on the evidence and not by the judge as a matter of law.

Even this clarification of the law did not succeed in making things clear to a jury, and it proved necessary for the Lord Chief Justice in the Court of Appeal to provide a model direction for a jury, to be used in those admittedly rare cases where the line between intention and recklessness was unclear.

Authority: *Nedrick* (1986). The defendant had pushed lighted materials through a letter box in order to frighten his victim, but realising that there was a serious risk of death. The facts were almost identical to the previous House of Lords authority, *Hyam*, which had not been specifically overruled by *Moloney* or *Hancock*, and the *Hyam* direction was used. The Court of Appeal overturned the murder conviction and set out guidelines in directing a jury, indicating that a jury should be told that if they found both that the consequence of death was a virtually certain result of the defendant's actions, and that he realised this, then they would find it very easy to infer intention as a question of fact from that evidence.

This definition, and the *Nedrick* direction where appropriate, are relevant to all offences, and not just murder.

Authority: *Walker and Hayles* (1990). Ds were charged with attempted murder. They dropped their victim from a third floor balcony, severely injuring him. They had previously threatened to kill him. The Court of Appeal held that intent had the same meaning for all offences, and there was no narrower definition applicable to attempts.

One of the reasons this area is so complex is because words are used which mean different things to lawyers and laymen, and even different things to different lawyers. The student who is confused should take comfort from the obvious fact that the judges are sometimes also confused. Added to this, some cases have very definite policy influences in them (*e.g. Steane*) and a case which may do individual justice can also cause confusion in judges and students for years to come. Sometimes there is no logical explanation.

Specific and basic intent

Matters are further complicated by a difference between crimes of "basic" intent and crimes of "specific" intent, the distinction between which similarly defies logical explanation.

Crimes of basic intent are those for which the *mens rea* can be either intention or recklessness.

Crimes of specific intent are crimes where only direct or oblique intent will suffice, or crimes where *mens rea* as to one element goes beyond the *actus reus* and requires something extra. Murder and attempts are examples of the first kind of specific intent offence. There are several examples of the second kind, mostly set out in statute. For example the definition of theft requires *an intent* permanently to deprive. Section 18 of the Offences against the Person Act covers wounding *with intent* to do grievous bodily harm, etc. These crimes require intention or recklessness with regard to the other parts of the *actus reus* but only intent will suffice with regard to that one element.

The reasons for the distinction between crimes of specific and crimes of basic intent stem from a series of policy decisions by the courts on the effect of intoxication in negativing *mens rea* (see Chap. 6).

It is sufficient to say in this context that one looks in vain for a logical distinction. The only sure way to know which crimes are in which category is to learn the lists, as the categorisation of certain crimes as one or the other has been influenced by the desire to convict someone who is obviously morally blameworthy but technically innocent. (See, *e.g. Majewski*, Chap. 6.)

Examples of crimes of specific intent are attempts, murder, theft, burglary, obtaining property by deception and wounding with intent.

Unlawful wounding, criminal damage, manslaughter, common assault, rape, and taking and driving away are crimes of basic intent.

RECKLESSNESS

The partial simplification of the law relating to intention brought about by the House of Lords in *Moloney* is but little compensation in comparison with the confusion caused by the decision in *Caldwell*. *Caldwell* has in effect created a new category of recklessness.

Recklessness is the taking of an unjustified risk. There are various factors which are relevant in deciding whether the risk is justified, and a jury would be expected to take into account:

   (i)   How likely it is that the risked consequences will occur.
   (ii) How socially useful the acts are.
   (iii) How easily precautions could be taken to avoid or minimise the risk.

"Cunningham" recklessness

Before *Caldwell*, it was generally agreed by case law and by academic opinion that the test for recklessness was subjective: *i.e.* the defendant must himself have realised the risk. It was not an objective test based on the standards of the reasonable man. Any liability based on those objective terms was classed as liability for negligence.

Authority: *Cunningham* (1957). This is the leading case on subjective recklessness. D was charged under section 23 of the Offences against the Person Act 1861 with "maliciously administering a noxious thing so as to endanger life." He had broken a gas meter to steal the money in it and the gas had seeped out into the next-door house. The victim became ill and her life was endangered. The Court of Appeal defined malice as requiring either intention or recklessness in the sense of the defendant himself having seen the risk and gone ahead with his act anyway.

"Caldwell" recklessness

The newer and much wider definition of recklessness is objective. It covers the situation where the risk is obvious to the reasonable man, in that any reasonable person would have realised it if he had thought about it. A person is reckless in the new wider sense when he gives no thought at all to the "obvious" risk, as well as if he thinks about it and decides to take it.

Authority: *Caldwell* (1981). D started a fire at his victim's hotel and caused some damage. Criminal damage is defined in the Criminal Damage Act 1971 in terms of either recklessness or intention. The House of Lords held that D was reckless as to whether he damaged property if he created *an obvious risk* of damage and either had not given any thought to the possibility of such a risk when he carried out the act in question or had recognised that there was some risk involved and nonetheless went on to carry it out.

Lord Diplock gave the leading speech. He felt that the person who does not stop to think is at least as culpable as the person who does stop to think and goes ahead with the risk.

Authority: *Lawrence* (1981). The decision in *Caldwell* was followed in *Lawrence*, a case of reckless driving. The House of Lords applied the same test of recklessness which they had applied in *Caldwell*. Their Lordships talked of an "obvious and serious risk." This was another statutory offence. "*Caldwell*" recklessness therefore applies to statutory offences where the *mens rea* includes recklessness.

The House of Lords has recently reconsidered the meaning of reckless-ness in the context of reckless driving. Their Lordships limited themselves to discussing recklessness under the Road Traffic Act 1972. However the speeches are long and detailed despite the fact that the Road Traffic Act 1991 which came into force on July 1, 1992 replaces the recklessness element in these offences with the concept of dangerousness. This might indicate that the more generalised comments on objective recklessness, approving Lord Diplock's explanation of the ordinary meaning of that word, might, although *obiter*, be important.

Authority: *Reid* (1992). D was trying to overtake on the nearside and struck a rest hut on the side of the road, killing his passenger. He was found guilty of causing death by reckless driving, applying the *Caldwell* recklessness test.

Authority: *Elliott* v. *C.* (1983). D was a 14 year old school girl in a remedial class at school. She set fire to a shed with some white spirit and matches. The magistrates found that she gave no thought to the risk of damage, and that even if she had, she would not have been capable of appreciating it. The Divisional Court held that this was irrelevant to the issue of recklessness. When the court in *Caldwell* had talked about an "obvious" risk, they had meant obvious to the reasonable man if he had thought about it, and not obvious to the defendant if *he* had thought about it.

The Caldwell "loophole"

Following *Caldwell* there was academic discussion about the breadth of *Caldwell* recklessness and whether it encompassed everything that had been referred to as negligence. An argument arose concerning the state of mind of the person who did give some thought to the risk involved in his actions but decided (wrongly and unreasonably) either that there was no risk at all, or that he had eliminated an existing risk completely, or that he had minimised it to an acceptable level. It could be argued that these states of mind did not come within the precise wording of Lord Diplock's definition, and therefore although such a defendant might be negligent he was not reckless. The only one of these possible "loopholes" to be specifi-cally tested is the last one.

Authority: *C.C. of Avon & Somerset Constabulary* v. *Shimmen* (1986). The defendant was a martial arts expert who was demonstrating his skill to friends by performing a move which he anticipated would bring his foot within inches of a shop window. He had miscalculated the risk, and he broke the window. The argument that he was not reckless because he had given thought to the risk but mistakenly believed he had minimised it, was rejected, and he was found guilty of causing criminal damage.

The House of Lords in *Reid* (above) did discuss the concept of a "loophole." Their opinion, although only *obiter*, was that there was no real loophole in the two stage definition. Either the evidence would be such that it would be almost impossible to convince a jury that D did not forsee the risk, or there would be some explanation of why he did not, which would either be irrelevant (*e.g.* intoxication), or would be such that it would take the behaviour out of the realms of "unjustified" risk taking. Examples are given, such as a sudden illness or shock. It is not clear how this fits in with the explanation of objective recklessness given in *Elliott* v. *C.* (above).

"Cunningham" or "Caldwell" recklessness?

Which offences are still based on "*Cunningham*" recklessness?

(i) Those like *Cunningham* where the word "maliciously" is used.

Authority: *W.* v. *Dalbey* (1983). D was charged under section 20 of the Offences against the Person Act 1861 with malicious wounding. His conviction was quashed by the Divisional Court becaue the magistrates had based their decision on the *Caldwell* definition of recklessness, and the Divisional Court said that in an offence under section 20, "*Cunningham*" recklessness should apply.

It is now clear from recent case law that *Cunningham* recklessness applies to assault and the offence under section 47 of the Offences Against the Person Act 1861.

Authority: *Savage, Parmenter* (1991). Ds in both cases were involved in assaults which caused harm. The main point at issue was the relevant *mens rea* required as to the act itself and as to the actual harm caused, in assault, section 47 and section 20 of the 1861 Act. The House of Lords held that where recklessness was the requisite *mens rea*, then that recklessness was subjective. There was no room for objective recklessness in any of these offences. (See further Chap. 7.)

(ii) Rape cases. Despite initial reaction that "*Caldwell*" recklessness applied in rape cases, a series of recent decisions has confirmed the view that this reaction was wrong. The Sexual Offences Act 1976 was passed specifically to give statutory effect to the decision in *D.P.P.* v. *Morgan* (1976) that an honest but unreasonable belief in the victim's consent will negative *mens rea* for rape, and this coincides with "*Cunningham*" recklessness.

Authority: *Satnam S.* (1984). The trial judge directed the jury on the basis of a risk obvious to the ordinary observer. This was held on appeal to be a misdirection. The Court of Appeal held that directions to juries on reckless rape should be on section 1 of the Sexual Offences Act 1976 and on *D.P.P.* v. *Morgan* and not on the basis of *Caldwell*.

Which offences are based on *"Caldwell"* recklessness?
1. Reckless driving and causing death by reckless driving (only relevant in respect of acts occurring before July 1, 1992).
2. Manslaughter.

Authority: *Seymour* (1983). D attempted to push a car off the road with his lorry. In doing so he crushed his victim between the two vehicles and she died. He was found guilty of manslaughter, the House of Lords affirming his conviction and stating that the *Caldwell* definition of recklessness applied to common law offences.

Since *Reid* (above), indicates a judicial approval of the objective concept of recklessness, in contrast to most academic opinion, evidenced by the Draft Criminal Code, in favour of completely subjective definition, the future development of the law appears to be uncertain.

NEGLIGENCE

Although as mentioned above (*Caldwell* "loophole" and *Reid*) it is not completely clear whether there is still a concept apart from recklessness called negligence, the uncertainty still necessitates a look at the traditional approach.

Negligence consists of a falling below the standard of the ordinary reasonable man, and either doing something he would not do, or not doing something which he would do. The test is objective, based on the hypothetical person, and not subjective, based on the defendant himself. Not all negligent behaviour is criminal. Liability depends on how far below the reasonable standard the defendant has fallen. In this respect the law refers to gross negligence.

The main crime based on negligence is manslaughter, although since *Seymour* decided that *"Caldwell"* recklessness should apply to manslaughter by an unlawful act, the importance of this as a separate head of liability has decreased.

BLAMELESS INADVERTENCE

A person is blamelessly inadvertent with regard to a consequence or circumstance if he did not realise that it might exist or occur, and no reasonable person would have so realised.

Crimes in which a person with this state of mind can be found guilty are referred to as crimes of strict liability, although the situation where a person can be found guilty of a criminal offence when he is blamelessly inadvertent with regard to all the elements of the *actus reus* are rare.

TRANSFERRED INTENT

The law says that the defendant will be liable for an offence if he has the necessary *mens rea* and commits the *actus reus* even if the victim differs from the one intended, or the consequence occurs in a different way.

Authority: *Latimer* (1886). D aimed a blow at one person with his belt. The belt recoiled off that person and hit the victim, who was severely injured. The court held that D was liable for maliciously wounding the victim. His malice was transferred from his intended to his unintended victim.

If the defendant has the *mens rea* for a different offence from that which he commits however, the intent cannot be transferred.

Authority: *Pembliton* (1874). D threw a stone at some people. He missed, and broke a window. The court held that he was not guilty of damaging the window as he had no *mens rea* for that offence and the *mens rea* for a completely different offence could not be transferred to make him liable.

COINCIDENCE OF *ACTUS REUS* AND *MENS REA*

One final problem in this area concerns the coincidence in time of the *actus reus* and the *mens rea*. The two must coincide for there to be criminal liability.

In some cases a literal interpretation of this rule would manifestly lead to injustice, and the courts have developed ways of finding coincidence of *actus reus* and *mens rea* when the events take place over a period of time, and constitute a course of events.

Continuing Acts

One way is to say that an *actus reus* in some circumstances involves a continuing act and a later *mens rea* can therefore coincide.

Authority: *Fagan* v. *Metropolitan Police Commissioner* (1969). D accidentally drove his car on to a policeman's foot and when he realised, he refused to remove it immediately. The court held that the *actus reus* of the assault was a continuing act in progress all the time the car was on the policeman's foot, so the subsequent *mens rea* could coincide with the *actus reus* at a later stage.

Authority: *Kaitamaki* (1984). D was charged with rape. His defence was that when he penetrated the woman he thought she was consenting. When he realised that she objected he did not withdraw. The Privy Council held that the *actus reus* of rape was a continuing act, and when he realised that she did not consent (and he therefore formed the necessary *mens rea*) the *actus reus* was still in progress and there could therefore be coincidence.

One transaction

The second way the courts have dealt with the problem is to consider a continuing series of acts to be "one transaction" for the purposes of the criminal law. If *actus reus* and *mens rea* are both present at some time during this transaction, then there is liability.

Authority: *Thabo Meli* v. *R.* (1954). Ds had attempted to kill their victim by beating him over the head. They threw the body over a cliff. He died from the fall and exposure, and not from the beating. The Privy Council held that this was all one series of acts following through a pre-conceived plan of action and therefore could not be seen as separate acts at all. *Actus reus* and *mens rea* were present during the transaction and therefore Ds were guilty of murder.

Authority: *Church* (1966). The same reasoning was applied here even where there was no pre-conceived plan and D, having killed (or so he thought) unexpectedly, disposed of the "body" in a panic and thereby caused death.

Authority: *Le Brun* (1991). D committed an initial assault and then unintentionally killed what he believed to be a corpse in trying to cover up his crime. The Court of Appeal confirmed and applied the reasoning in *Church*.

This kind of reasoning should be recognised for what it is: a way to avoid a logical but unjust result.

Reforms

The Draft Criminal Code replaces the phrase *mens rea* with the concept of fault. Fault is defined in terms of knowledge, intention and recklessness.

A person has knowledge of a circumstance if they are aware it exists or they avoid taking steps to confirm their belief in its existence (the equivalent of "wilful blindness").

A person intends a circumstance if he knows of or hopes for its existence. He intends a result if he acts in order to bring it about or is aware it will occur in the ordinary course of events.

A person is reckless if he is aware of a risk that the circumstance exists or that a result will occur and it is unreasonable in the circumstances as they are known to him to take that risk.

These definitions show an attempt to clarify existing concepts with the exception of the definition of recklessness which involves a positive move back to subjective recklessness. *Caldwell* recklessness as a basis for liability would be completely abolished under these proposals.

Most recently the Law Commission Consultation Paper (No. 122, 1992), in clause 25, reaffirms the principle of transferred fault. The clause incorporates transferred intent, but refers to "awareness of risk" rather than using the term "recklessness."

The clause also confirms that defences applicable in relation to the person or thing in D's contemplation can similarly be "transferred."

SUMMARY

The main topics for revision are:

Intention
   (*Steane*)
   Direct and Oblique Intent (*Moloney*)
   The Law Post-*Moloney* (*Moloney, Hancock, Nedrick, Walker and Hayles*)
   Specific and Basic Intent (*examples*)

Recklessness
   "*Cunningham*" Recklessness (*Cunningham*)
   "*Caldwell*" Recklessness (*Caldwell, Lawrence, Reid, Elliott* v. *C., Seymour*)
   The *Caldwell* "loophole" (*Shimmen, Reid*)
   "*Cunningham*" or "*Caldwell*" Recklessness? Lists for each (*W.* v. *Dalbey*, *Satnam S., Reid*)

Negligence

Blameless inadvertence
   Crimes of strict liability

Transferred intent
   (*Latimer, Pembliton*)

Coincidence of *actus reus* and *mens rea*
   Continuing Acts (*Fagan, Kaitamaki*)
   One Transaction (*Thabo Meli, Church, Le Brun*)

Reforms
   Draft Criminal Code
   Law Commission Consultation Paper

---

3. STRICT LIABILITY

WHAT IS STRICT LIABILITY?

There are some crimes for which, with regard to at least one element of the *actus reus*, *e.g.* a particular circumstance or required consequence, no *mens rea* is required. The defendant need not have intended or known about that circumstance or consequence. Liability is said to be strict with regard to that element.

It is untrue to say that crimes of strict liability never require *mens rea*. *Mens rea* may well be required with regard to other elements of the *actus reus*. It is only in extreme and rare cases where no *mens rea* is required for liability, thereby making the particular offence "absolute."

Authority: *Larsonneur* (1933), and *Winzar* v. *Chief Constable of Kent* (1983). (See Chap. 1.)

Most strict liability crimes therefore are only "strict" as to one element of the *actus reus*.

Authority: *Prince* (1875). D was considered guilty of an offence under what is now section 20 of the Sexual Offences Act 1956 of unlawfully taking an unmarried girl under the age of 16 years out her parent's possession. He had run off with a girl whom he honestly and reasonably believed to be 18. The prohibited act consists of abducting the girl, one required circumstance being that it was against her parent's will, and another being that she was under 16. D has to have *mens rea* with regard to all the elements of the *actus reus* except the circumstance that she is under 16. This is what makes it an offence of strict liability.

COMMON LAW STRICT LIABILITY OFFENCES

The vast majority of strict liability crimes are statutory offences, but some are common law offences. Public nuisance is one common law example and blasphemous libel another.

STATUTORY STRICT LIABILITY OFFENCES

There is a presumption that *mens rea* is an essential ingredient in any offence. However the courts have proved willing to displace that presumption in a variety of cases and impose strict liability, although their attitudes have fluctuated over the years.

There are two types of offence where the courts have been willing to impose strict liability. (See *Gammon (Hong Kong) Ltd.* v. *Attorney General*, below.)

Regulatory offences

One kind is the purely regulatory offence where no moral issue is at stake, the penalty is small, and from a practical point of view strict liability makes it easier to enforce these offences. Legislation relating to the sale of food provides a good example of this category. (See, *e.g. Smedleys Ltd.* v. *Breed*, below.)

Public danger offences

The second kind of offence is where the protection of the public is paramount. Here the penalty may be severe but strict liability is still felt necessary to induce the highest standard of care. The pollution cases are an example of this category, as are the dangerous drugs cases.

Authority: *Warner* v. *Metropolitan Police Commissioner* (1968). D was charged with being in possession of a prohibited drug contrary to section 1 of the (now repealed) Drugs (Prevention of Misuse) Act 1964. He had been given two boxes, one containing perfume and the other the drug. He said he thought they both contained perfume. The House of Lords held that *mens rea* was necessary regarding the possession, but not regarding the knowledge that what he possessed was a dangerous drug: as long as D knew he possessed the container with something in it, it did not matter that he did not know, and could not reasonably have known, that the contents were a prohibited drug.

A limited defence now exists under the Misuse of Drugs Act 1971, if a defendant can show that he did not know or suspect, and could not reasonably have known or suspected, that the substance was a prohibited drug. This, it can be argued, is equivalent to importing fault in the form of negligence, and may indicate a change in attitude towards this kind of strict liability offence, as does the next case.

Authority: *Sweet* v. *Parsley* (1969). D was a landlady who did not live on the premises, but only visited occasionally. Her lodgers smoked cannabis and she was charged with being concerned in the management of premises which were used for the purposes of smoking cannabis contrary to section 5 of the (now repealed) Dangerous Drugs Act 1965. It was not proved that she knew of the smoking. The magistrates and the Divisional Court held that no *mens rea* was necessary for this element of the *actus reus* and found her guilty.

The House of Lords on further appeal quashed the conviction and said that this was not an offence of strict liability. Lord Reid re-stated the general principle that where a statute says nothing about *mens rea*, it will be assumed that *mens rea* will be required. If Parliament wishes to create a crime of strict liability then it must make its intention manifest.

His Lordship also made the basic distinction between crimes which were truly criminal, where penalties were severe and *mens rea* should be required, and purely regulatory offences with minor penalties. These offences were "quasi-criminal" and strict liability was a practical and acceptable way of dealing with them. This explains one kind of strict liability offence, but not the "protection of the public" type of offence. This explanation should be compared with the later one in *Gammon Ltd.* v. *Attorney General* (see below).

SOME AREAS OF STRICT LIABILITY OFFENCES

There is no foolproof way of spotting in advance a strict liability crime, but there are certain kinds of offence, and certain types of wording used in statutes, which are more likely to lead to the imposition of strict liability.

Dangerous drugs

There are several crimes concerning dangerous drugs where liability is strict. These offences fall into the category of protection of public safety.

Authority: *Warner* v. *Metropolitan Police Commissioner*. (See above.)

The new legislation since *Warner* is the Misuse of Drugs Act 1971.

Authority: *Marriott* (1971). D was in possession of a penknife which he knew had traces of a substance on it. This substance turned out to be a prohibited drug. The court held that D needed *mens rea* with regard to possession of a substance on the knife, but not *mens rea* with regard to the circumstance that the substance was a prohibited drug. It did not matter that he did not know, and could not reasonably have known, what the substance was.

However, this general policy of protection in the dangerous drugs cases has its limits.

Authority: *Sweet* v. *Parsley*. (See above.)

Road traffic offences

Some road traffic offences where strict liability is imposed are of a regulatory, quasi-criminal nature while others are more serious.

Authority: *Bowsher* (1973). Where D was convicted of driving while disqualified even when he believed his disqualification had ended, and reasonably believed this because his licence had been returned to him.

Another example is the offence of driving with an amount of alcohol in the bloodstream which is over the prescribed limit, contrary to section 5 of the Road Traffic Act 1988. *Mens rea* is not required with regard to the circumstances of having an amount of alcohol in the bloodstream over the prescribed limit.

Pollution

Crimes involving pollution often provide other examples of strict liability crimes designed to protect the public.

Authority: *Alphacell Ltd.* v. *Woodward* (1972). D was charged with causing polluted matter to enter a river contrary to section 2 of the Rivers (Prevention of Pollution) Act 1951. The river had in fact been polluted because a pipe had been blocked, and the defendants had not been negligent. The House of Lords nevertheless held that the defendants were liable. The Law Lords indicated that to introduce a *mens rea* requirement would lower the standard of care and increase the amount of pollution generally.

Sale of food

This is another regulatory area which, given the number of cases and the work of the inspectorate, it is felt is best kept under control by strict liability.

Authority: *Smedleys Ltd.* v. *Breed* (1974). D company was charged with selling food which is not of the substance demanded by the purchaser. A caterpillar had been found in a tin of peas from D company's factory. The House of Lords held D liable even though there were no other practicable preventive measures which could have been taken, and the standard of care taken at the factory was extremely high.

There are other areas where strict liability is prevalent, for example trade and industry, public health and liquor regulations.

DEFENCES

Some statutes imposing so-called strict liability now contain a limited form of defence, often based on lack of negligence. It can be argued that this trend is turning crimes of strict liability into crimes of negligence. Whether one considers this desirable depends on how strongly one is convinced of the arguments for and against strict liability (see below).

Dangerous drugs

There is a defence under section 28 to offences against the Misuse of Drugs Act 1971, if the *defendant* can prove that he neither knew of nor suspected, nor had reason to suspect, the existence of some fact which the prosecution have to prove for the offence to be committed.

Sale of food

Under section 21 of the Food Act 1990, D has a defence if he took all reasonable precautions and exercised all due diligence to avoid the commission of the offence by himself or a person under his control. This in effect is a "no negligence" defence with the burden of proof on the defendant to show that he was not negligent.

ARGUMENTS FOR AND AGAINST STRICT LIABILITY

The main issues in this topic are ones of policy. The basis for almost any examination question will therefore be an appreciation of the arguments in favour of and against strict liability as a concept.

Arguments in favour

The main reasons for imposing strict liability are;

(a) to protect the public from dangerous actions by creating a higher standard of care, and

(b) to regulate quasi-criminal activities in as efficient a manner as possible.

Authority: *Gammon (Hong Kong) Ltd.* v. *Attorney General* (1984). In which the arguments in favour of strict liability are clearly set out.

This was an example of a regulatory offence concerning breach of building regulations. The Privy Council held that although there is a presumption of *mens rea* to be read into all statutes, this can be displaced on clear evidence in two kinds of case:

(i) Cases of public protection where social danger exists.

(ii) Quasi-criminal offences of a regulatory nature.

The reasons for displacing the requirement of *mens rea* in such cases were said to be the encouraging of a higher standard of vigilance, and ease of administration.

(c) to facilitate the investigation and control of corporate crime. Crimes committed by corporations are often under-reported and under-prosecuted, despite the consequences, both in terms of money and life. The prosecution of a corporation for manslaughter following the Zeebrugge ferry disaster is almost unprecedented. The imposition of strict liability can help the control of corporate crime because it dispenses in some respects with the often difficult task of imputing the necessary *mens rea* to a sufficiently senior official within a corporation.

Arguments against

The arguments against strict liability are basically answers to the above.

It is disputed whether imposing strict liability does ensure a higher standard of care. It is difficult to prove or disprove the statement. Equally arguable is the following: if one knows that however reasonably, not to say vigilantly, one behaves, one can still be guilty of a criminal offence, then the incentive to take all reasonable care is reduced rather than increased.

The practical and administrative arguments in favour of strict liability are also disputed on practical grounds.

Cases still have to be detected and brought to court, and some elements of the *mens rea* still have to be proved. The degree of negligence is still also relevant in the sentencing, so evidence of it must be available. Given all this it is difficult to see how much time and manpower is actually saved.

However, the main argument against strict liability is one of principle, and not a practical one. It is objectionable in principle to impose an unreasonably high standard of behaviour on people by means of punishing them for its absence under the criminal law. However slight the punishment there is a stigma attached to a criminal conviction which should not attach to a person who has taken all reasonable care.

REFORMS

The trend away from strict liability evidenced by the speeches in *Sweet* v. *Parsley* and by the introduction of statutory defences is apparent.

In Australia offences of strict liability have been mitigated by allowing a defence of all due care, a burden being on the defendant to prove his defence. This is one approach we have started to follow in this country and which could be more generally adopted.

This is not an area which attracts a lot of publicity or debate. Although many people think that there should be no strict liability, and a minimum fault element of negligence should be required, others think the system works well in its present state, and the administrative benefits outweigh any objections. Any major reform is unlikely.

SUMMARY

The main topics for revision are:

What is strict liability?
(*Larsonneur*, *Winzar* v. *Chief Constable of Kent*, *Prince*)

Common law strict liability offences

Statutory strict liability offences
(*Gammon* v. *A.G.*)
Regulatory Offences (*Smedleys* v. *Breed*)
Public Danger Offences (*Warner* v. *M.P.C.*, *Sweet* v. *Parsley*)

Some areas of strict liability offences
Dangerous Drugs (*Warners* v. *M.P.C.*, *Marriott*, *Sweet* v. *Parsley*)
Road Traffic Offences (*Bowsher*, Road Traffic Act 1972, s.6)
Pollution (*Alphacell* v. *Woodward*)
Sale of Food (*Smedleys* v. *Breed*)

Defences
Dangerous Drugs (Misuse of Drugs Act 1971)
Sale of Food (Food Safety Act 1990)

Arguments for and against strict liability
In Favour:
Protection of the Public
Administration of Regulatory Offences
(*Gammon* v. *A.G.*)
Control of corporate crime

Against:
No higher standard of care
No saving in administration
Bad principle to impose unreasonably high standard of care

Reforms
Australian System.

---

4. PARTIES TO CRIME

It is not only the perpetrator who will be liable for a criminal offence. If other persons participate in the offence they too may be liable.

Under section 8 of the Accessories and Abettors Act 1861 as amended by the Criminal Law Act 1967:

> "Whosoever shall *aid, abet, counsel or procure* the commission of any indictable offence, whether the same be an offence at common law or by virtue of any Act passed or to be passed, shall be liable to be tried, indicted and punished as a principal offender."

Section 44 of the Magistrates' Courts Act 1980 makes a similar provision with respect to summary offences. Those involved in crimes to a lesser degree in this way are referred to as secondary parties and as a general rule their liability is the same as that of the principal. However, where there is a discretion in sentencing their degree of involvement will be taken into account.

An offence must actually have been committed before anyone can be liable as a secondary party.

PRINCIPALS

Joint principals
The principal is the main perpetrator of the offence: the one who commits the *actus reus* or the substantial part of the *actus reus*. It is possible to have more than one principal if more than one person is directly responsible for the *actus reus*. The test is whether someone contributes to the *actus reus* by his own independent act rather than merely aiding or abetting.

Innocent agents
A principal may not always directly carry out the *actus reus* himself. He may use an innocent agent.

SECONDARY PARTICIPATION

There are four kinds of secondary participation:
- (i) Aiding,
- (ii) Abetting,
- (iii) Counselling,
- (iv) Procuring.

These four words have been held to have distinct meanings, although aiding and abetting are often charged together, as are counselling and procuring.

Authority: *Attorney General's Reference No. 1 of 1975.* The principal offender was driving with a blood-alcohol level over the prescribed limit. The secondary party had added alcohol to the principal's drink without his knowledge, knowing that he would be driving. Some general comments were made about secondary participation, and the distinctions between the four modes of secondary participation.

Aiding

This is defined as helping the principal at the time he commits the offence. As long as help is given, there is no need to establish any causal link or even the knowledge of the principal.

Abetting

Abetting indicates a more positive involvement amounting to encouragement or incitement, and normally takes place at the time of the offence. It implies an element of co-operation which indicates the principal's knowledge and agreement.

Counselling

This also involves giving advice and encouragement and closely resembles abetting, but whereas the concept of abetting seems confined to the scene of the crime, counselling takes place beforehand.

Authority: *Calhaem* (1985). D was charged with murder. She was said to have counselled Z to commit murder. Z gave evidence that despite D's instructions he had no intention of carrying out the killing. However, when he got to the victim's flat he had gone "berserk" and killed her. The jury was directed that counselling involved "putting somebody up to something" and that the acts carried out must be within the scope of the instructions. D was convicted and appealed on the basis that the jury should have been directed that there had to be a causal connection between the counselling and the act, and here there was not. The court held that there was no requirement of a causal connection in counselling, and the conviction was affirmed.

Procuring

This means to "produce by endeavour." It is unnecessary for the principal to know about the procuring, but procuring does imply a causal connection.

Authority: *Attorney General's Reference No. 1 of 1975.* This was a case where the procuring was without the knowledge and consent of the principal but was the cause of the offence (see above).

ASSISTANCE AFTER THE COMMISSION OF AN ARRESTABLE OFFENCE

Assistance given after the commission of the offence, to enable someone to escape or dispose of evidence or proceeds for example, does not come within the definitions of aiding, abetting, counselling or procuring. It is a separate offence intentionally to impede the apprehension or prosecution of an arrestable offender under section 4 of the Criminal Law Act 1967.

PRESENCE AT THE SCENE OF THE CRIME

Merely witnessing an offence and omitting to try to stop or report it does not amount to secondary participation.

Authority: *Coney* (1882). D was present at a bare fists prize fight. The court held that presence at a crime does not constitute secondary participation in it as a matter of law. It is simply one factor for a jury to take into account. However, if there is evidence of any other supportive activity it is much more likely that liability will arise.

Authority: *Wilcox* v. *Jeffrey* (1951). D was present at a concert given by someone who was performing in the country in contravention of the Aliens Order 1920. He had met the performer at the airport beforehand and later praised the performance in a magazine. The court held that this was sufficient evidence of encouragement to constitute secondary participation.

PARTICIPATION BY OMISSION

Failing to prevent an offence can amount to participating in it where a person is in a position to prevent it because he is in control of property or for some other reason.

Authority: *Tuck* v. *Robinson* (1970). D was the licensee of a public house. He allowed his customer to drink after hours and thereby commit offences. His inactivity was held to constitute aiding and abetting because he was in a position of authority and control, and therefore under a duty to act.

Authority: *Bland* (1987). The appellant lived with someone who was guilty of possession of drugs. She was found guilty of aiding and abetting him, but the conviction was quashed on appeal. The court found that there was no evidence of active or passive assistance. Living in the same room was not enough.

MENS REA OF SECONDARY PARTIES

Knowledge

Secondary participants need both *mens rea* as to their own *actus reus* and knowledge, or at least wilful blindness, of the circumstances of the offence. This is so even in relation to strict liability offences.

Authority: *Callow* v. *Tillstone* (1900). D was a veterinary surgeon who had examined a carcass and negligently certified it as sound. The principal was strictly liable for selling unfit food, but D's conviction as a secondary participant was quashed because he had been merely negligent and had not *known* that the meat was unsound.

The secondary party need not know all the details of the offence to be committed but he must have an idea of the type of offence or have a series of possible offences in mind.

Authority: *Bainbridge* (1960). D had purchased some oxygen-cutting equipment on behalf of a third party who he knew was going to use it for an illegal purpose, although he was not sure what that purpose was. The court held that D, to be liable, would need to know more than that the purpose was illegal. Although he did not need to know all the details he would need to know, for example, that it was going to be used for breaking and entering.

Authority: *D.P.P. for Northern Ireland* v. *Maxwell* (1978). D was a member of a terrorist organisation. He was told to take some men to a cinema. He knew that their purpose was illegal but he did not know the specific details. He found out later that they had planted a bomb and was convicted of abetting an act done with intent to cause an unlawful explosion. The House of Lords held that he did not need to know the precise weapon and method to be used by the others. He knew they were terrorists. He knew their purpose would be to endanger life or property. That was enough.

This is even more general than *Bainbridge*, and widens the scope of liability.

Where the offence is procuring the commission of a crime, there is *obiter dicta* to the effect that recklessness as to whether the principal will commit the crime, is not sufficient *mens rea* for the secondary party.

Authority: *Blakely, Sutton* (1991). Ds had spiked their victim's drink intending to tell him before he left to drive home. In fact he left before they had a chance to tell him. He was stopped by police and eventually charged with driving with an excess of alcohol in the bloodstream. Ds here contended that they had never intended that he commit such an offence and they had not realised that he might leave before they could tell him what they had done. On appeal their convictions were quashed. The Court held that they were only reckless in the objective sense, and that was not enough for liability. Although not necessary for the decision, their Lordships expressed the opinion that only intention should suffice.

Unforeseen consequences

The secondary party is liable to the same extent as the principal for the consequences which flow from the agreed or authorised acts, whether they are foreseen or not. However, if one party goes beyond what is authorised or agreed then he alone will be liable for the resultant consequences.

Authority: *Anderson and Morris* (1966). Both Ds were involved in a fight with the victim. The first D had a knife and used it to kill the victim. The second D denied having the knife. He appealed against a conviction for manslaughter. The court held that if one party goes beyond what has been previously agreed and does something completely unexpected, then it is outside the common purpose and the other party is not liable. D's conviction was quashed.

If the secondary participant had in fact contemplated a different offence, with a different *actus reus* which does not occur, then he will not be liable for any offence.

Authority: *Dunbar* (1988). D was convicted of manslaughter and her co-defendants of murder. D appealed. She admitted that she knew her co-defendants planned to burgle the victim's flat and that some violence might be done to the victim, but she did not contemplate the possibility of any serious harm being inflicted. The Court of Appeal quashed her conviction. She had not contemplated the possibility of grievous bodily harm, and therefore could not be a secondary participant to murder. She only contemplated the possibility of causing actual bodily harm, and that offence was never committed. There was therefore no liability.

Joint enterprise

A secondary participant taking part in a joint enterprise will be liable for an offence committed by the principal if either they have expressly or impliedly agreed that the principal might commit the offence, or the secondary participant foresaw the possibility that the principal might so act, and he continued with the enterprise anyway.

Authority: *Chan Wing-Siu* (1985). The three Ds were charged with murder. They had gone armed with knives to the victim's flat supposedly to obtain payment of a debt. They said they had acted in self-defence in killing him. The third D denied knowledge of the knife. The Privy Council held that the parties were liable if they contemplated the possibility of really serious injury or death. A defendant could only escape liability if he had considered the risk so negligible as not to be worth thinking about, and in that sense it could be said to be unforeseen.

This was confirmed, following some disagreement and uncertainty in the case law, by two Court of Appeal decisions, *Slack* (1989) and *Hyde* (1991), and most recently by the Privy Council.

Authority: *Hui Chi-ming* (1991). Four people, including D, set upon the victim. One of them (not D) struck the fatal blow. D was liable for murder because even though there was no agreement between the parties, he had contemplated the possibility of serious injury or death. The Privy Council confirmed the law as set out in *Chan Wing-siu*.

ACQUITTAL OF PRINCIPAL OFFENDER

If there is no principal offender this does not necessarily present a problem. Providing it can be proved that an offence was committed, a secondary participant can be convicted.

The situation is more complicated if a principal offender is acquitted. Such an acquittal does not necessarily mean that no offence has been committed and therefore the above reasoning can be applied and secondary participants convicted.

No actus reus of an offence

What if the acquittal of a principal offender means that no offence has been committed? If no offence has been committed then there cannot be secondary liability.

Authority: *Thornton* v. *Mitchell* (1940). A conductor of a bus was charged as a secondary party to careless driving after helping a driver to reverse. The driver was acquitted on the basis of no carelessness. The conductor was acquitted too. If there was no carelessness then there was no offence to be aided and abetted.

Acquittal for other reasons

If there is an *actus reus* then there can be liability even if the alleged principal offender is not guilty for some other reason, *e.g.* no *mens rea* or a valid defence.

Authority: *Bourne* (1952). D forced his wife to commit buggery with a dog. The wife had acted under duress and was therefore not liable as a principal offender, but because an *actus reus* had been committed D could be, and was, liable as a secondary party.

Authority: *Cogan and Leak* (1976). D had persuaded a friend to have intercourse with his (D's) wife. The friend had honestly but unreasonably believed the wife was consenting and was therefore not guilty of rape. However, the *actus reus* of rape had been committed so it was possible for a secondary party who had not believed in the wife's consent to be liable. Such was D, but he was also her husband and a husband could not then be found guilty of raping his wife. The court tried to get around this problem by basing his conviction on the use of an innocent agent. This not only does not solve the problem of whether a husband can be liable as a secondary party to his wife's rape, but it creates the problem of finding the husband guilty as a principal.

A husband can now be guilty as a principal of rape of his wife (see *R.* (1992), Chap. 7).

LIABILITY OF SECONDARY PARTY FOR A DIFFERENT OFFENCE

A secondary party can be convicted of a less serious offence than the principal in circumstances where both offences have the same *actus reus* but a different *mens rea*. If however the principal has committed a different *actus reus*, that will not be the case (see *Dunbar*, above).

Similarly a secondary party may be convicted of a more serious offence where the situation in respect of *mens rea* is reversed.

Authority: *Hui Chi-ming* (1991). (See above for facts.) D was convicted as a secondary participant to murder because death had occurred and he had the requisite *mens rea* of a secondary participant to murder, as explained above. The Privy Council held that it was irrelevant that the principal had been convicted of manslaughter, rather than murder, as the *actus reus* was the same for both offences.

REPENTANCE OF SECONDARY PARTY

If an alleged secondary party repents before the offence is committed then he may escape liability if he repents at a sufficiently early stage and does all he reasonably can to avert commission of the crime.

Authority: *Becerra* (1976). D had agreed with his co-burglar that he should use a knife if anyone interrupted them, but when someone did approach he changed his mind, said "Let's go" and ran off. The other burglar used the knife and caused injury. The court held that the words were not sufficient withdrawal in themselves. More was needed, such as attempting to take away the knife.

What constitutes effective repentance depends on the facts of each case and is for the jury to decide.

VICTIMS AS SECONDARY PARTICIPANTS

Some statutes are passed specifically for the protection of a group of people, *e.g.* minors. Such persons will not be liable for any involvement in the criminal offence committed under the state.

Authority: *Tyrell* (1894). D was not guilty of aiding or abetting a male person in committing, or inciting him to commit, the misdemeanor of having unlawful carnal knowledge of her (a girl between the ages of 13 and 16) contrary to section 5 of the Criminal Law Amendment Act 1885. Although it was not disputed that she did so aid, abet and incite, she had not committed a criminal offence because the Act was passed for the purpose of protecting girls of that age and it was obviously not intended that they should be prosecuted.

CORPORATE LIABILITY

Corporations, such as limited companies, are legal entities, but there are obvious problems regarding their participation in a criminal offence as regards *mens rea*.

Although they cannot, practically speaking, form any necessary *mens rea*, criminal liability is imposed upon corporations and it covers more than the normal vicarious liability situations.

Liability is imposed on corporations in one of two ways:

Vicarious liability

A corporation is vicariously liable for the acts of its employees or agents in normal situations of vicarious liability (see below).

Persons in control

If certain key persons involved in the company, who control and direct the company's activities, commit a crime within the course of business, then for the purposes of the law that crime is also committed by the company.

Authority: *Tesco Supermarkets* v. *Nattrass* (1972). The D company was charged with an offence under the Trade Descriptions Act 1968. The actual omission was the responsibility of a branch manager, and the issue was whether he was a sufficiently key person to represent the company by his acts. The House of Lords held that he was not. Only persons who "carry out the functions of management and speak and act as the company" will represent the company in this way and make the company itself liable. Thus the larger the company the more difficult it may be to convict it of a non-vicarious offence.

In June 1989 the Director of Public Prosecutions announced that he would be bringing charges against both particular personnel and against the company itself in relation to the sinking of the Herald of Free Enterprise at Zeebrugge.

Authority: *P and O European Ferries (Dover) Ltd.* (1991). The Company and employees directly involved in the Zeebrugge disaster were jointly charged with manslaughter. The trial judge made it clear that there was no reason in principle why a corporation could not be found liable for manslaughter, but the prosecution failed because of difficulties in proving the requisite negligence. Charges against the individual employees were then also dropped.

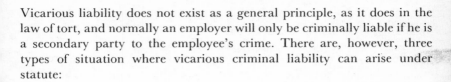

VICARIOUS LIABILITY

Vicarious liability does not exist as a general principle, as it does in the law of tort, and normally an employer will only be criminally liable if he is a secondary party to the employee's crime. There are, however, three types of situation where vicarious criminal liability can arise under statute:

Express vicarious liability

For example section 165 of the Licensing Act 1964 provides:

> "If any person in licensed premises himself *or by his servant or agent* sells or supplies to any person as the measure of intoxicating liquor for which he asks an amount exceeding that measure, he shall be liable to a fine . . ."

Delegated management

Where an employer is under a statutory duty, and delegates that duty to an employee, he will be vicariously liable for any criminal offence — even one requiring *mens rea* — which the employee "commits" while carrying out that duty.

Authority: *Allen* v. *Whitehead* (1930). D was charged with an offence of knowingly permitting prostitutes to meet together and remain in a place where refreshments are sold. D owned a cafe which was run by a manager. The manager knew about the prostitutes but D did not. The court held that D was vicariously liable because he had delegated his statutory duty and that meant that his manager's *actus reus* and *mens rea* were imputed to him.

This analogous form of liability is normally confined to licensees and offences under the Licensing Act 1964.

Vicarous liability implied by statute

The final situation where vicarious criminal liability will apply is more far-reaching, as express delegation is not required. This occurs where a statutory prohibition can fairly be interpreted as covering both an employee and his employer. This is common in strict liability "selling" offences, *e.g.* under the Food Safety Act 1990 and the Trade Descriptions Act 1968.

Authority: *Coppen* v. *Moore* (1898). D owned several shops where he sold American ham, described on his instructions as breakfast ham. One of his managers disobeyed him and sold it described as Scotch ham. This was a false trade description and therefore an offence. The court held that D, as the employer, had "sold" the ham, even though the transaction was carried out by his employee.

This would apply in a large supermarket, for example, or a department store: employee and employer are joint principals.

Reforms

Despite recognising that there were difficulties and inconsistences with the law relating to secondary participation, the Law Commission was unwilling to recommend any major reform without the benefit of a specific Working Party having undertaken a review of the area. This is in line with its general policy in drafting the Code.

The Code does however provide for the abolition of vicarious criminal liability under the delegated management principle.

SUMMARY

The main topics for revision are:

Principals
Joint Principals
Innocent Agents

Secondary participation
(*A.G.'s Ref. No 1 of 1975*)
Aiding
Abetting
Counselling (*Calhaem*)
Procuring (*A.G.'s Ref. No. 1 of 1975*)

Assistance after the commission of an arrestable offence

Presence at the scene of the crime
(*Coney Wilcox* v. *Jeffrey*)

Participation by omission
(*Tuck* v. *Robinson*)
(*Bland*)

Mens rea of secondary parties
Knowledge
(*Callow* v. *Tillstone, Bainbridge, D.P.P. for Northern Ireland* v. *Maxwell, Blakely and Sutton*)
Unforeseen Consequences
(*Anderson and Morris, Dunbar*)

Joint enterprise
(*Chan Wing-siu, Hui Chi-ming*)

Acquittal of principal offender
No *Actus Reus* of an Offence
(*Thornton* v. *Mitchell*)
Acquittal for Other Reasons
(*Bourne, Cogan and Leak*)

Liability of secondary party for a different offence
(*Hui Chi-ming*)

Repentance of secondary party
(*Becerra*)

Victims as secondary parties
(*Tyrell*)

Corporate liability
Vicarious Liability
Persons in Control (*Tesco* v. *Nattrass*, P & O European Ferries (Dover) Ltd.)

Vicarious liability
Express Vicarious Liability
Delegated Management (*Allen* v. *Whitehead*)
Vicarious Liability Implied by Statute (*Coppen* v. *Moore*)

Reforms
Draft Criminal Code. Abolition of vicarious liability by virtue of delegated management.

---

5. INCHOATE OFFENCES

The inchoate offences cover the preparatory stages of other criminal offences. They are substantive offences in themselves and, unlike liability for secondary participation in a crime, it is unnecessary that the main offence be committed. Indeed it is often unlikely, and in some cases impossible, that it will be.

There are three inchoate offences: incitement, conspiracy and attempt.

INCITEMENT

An inciter is someone who tries to help, influence, encourage, threaten or pressurise another party to commit a crime. The crime incited may or may not have actually been committed; it is irrelevant to the liability of the inciter, except that he may become a secondary participant if it has been committed.

Mens rea of incitement

All the inchoate offences are crimes of specific intent (see Chap. 2), and recklessness is therefore not sufficient *mens rea*; intention is necessary with regard to the consequences, and knowledge or belief with regard to the circumstances.

Inciting the impossible

This is governed by the common law and not by statute. There can be liability for incitement to do the impossible only if the commission of the crime was possible at the time of the incitement.

Authority: *Fitzmaurice* (1983). D's father had asked D to recruit people to commit a robbery. D recruited one person who recruited two others, and D put them in touch with his father. Unknown to D, no crime was to be committed at all. It was a plan of his father's to claim reward money for preventing a robbery.

D was convicted of incitement to rob. The person he recruited had already been acquitted of conspiracy on the grounds of impossibility. The Court of Appeal said that the fact that conspiracy had been impossible did not necessarily mean that the incitement would be. The offence he had incited had not itself been impossible to commit at the time he incited it, and therefore he was liable. He would not have been liable had it been physically impossible at any time. The law was therefore in line with the old common law on conspiracy and attempt, and not in line with the new rules in those areas enacted by the Criminal Law Act 1977 and the Criminal Attempts Act 1981.

The previous case of *McDonough* is explained in line with this reasoning and the previous wide interpretation of liability for impossible incitements is questionable.

CONSPIRACY

A conspiracy is an agreement by two or more persons to either commit a crime or to defraud someone or to corrupt public morals. The limits of conspiracy are controlled by the Criminal Law Act 1977, which left the latter two categories intact only as a temporary measure, as major reforms in those areas were being considered. Conspiracy is therefore governed partly by the common law and partly by statute.

Statutory conspiracy

Under section 1(1) of the Criminal Law Act 1977:

> "Subject to the following provisions of this Part of this Act, if a person agrees with any other person or persons that a course of conduct shall be pursued which, if the agreement is carried out in accordance with their intentions, either—
> (a) will necessarily amount to or involve the commission of any offence or offences by one or more of the parties to the agreement, or—
> (b) would do so but for the existence of facts which render the commission of the offence or any of the offences impossible,
>
> he is guilty of conspiracy to commit the offence or offences in question."

Under section 1(2):

> "Where liability for any offence may be incurred without knowledge on the part of the person committing it of any particular fact or circumstances necessary for the commission of the offence, a person shall nevertheless not be guilty of conspiracy to commit that offence by virtue of subsection (1) above unless he and at least one other party to the agreement intend or know that that fact or circumstances shall or will exist at the time when the conduct constituting the offence is to take place."

These subsections make it clear that the *mens rea* for conspiracy is intention only and not recklessness. Knowledge or belief is required as to circumstances, not merely suspicion, even with respect to crimes of strict liability. Conspiracy is therefore a crime of specific intent.

Conspiracies to commit criminal offences are therefore covered by section 1 of the Act, and are often referred to as "section 1 conspiracies."

This section has however been the subject of interpretation by the House of Lords which has left the matter in some confusion.

Authority: *Anderson* (1986). D had agreed to supply wire-cutters to be used in a gaol break, but claimed that he never intended the plan to go ahead, and did not believe it would succeed. The House of Lords held that it was not necessary for liability that he intended the plan to go ahead. Therefore there could theoretically be a conspiracy even when none of the conspirators ever intend the plan to be put into action. The House of Lords held *obiter dicta* that a defendant would only be guilty of conspiracy if he planned to play some active part in the carrying out of the agreement. This had not generally been thought to be the law, and it may be that as an *obiter* statement it will be disregarded.

The Court of Appeal took the opportunity to "explain" this *mens rea* requirement, by saying that an intention to participate in the furtherance of the crime can be shown simply by failure to stop the criminal acts.

Authority: *Siracusa* (1989). The conspiracy involved agreements to import heroin and cannabis into the country. Although it was not necessary for the *ratio* of the case, the Court's confirmation that there can be a passive as well as an active conspiracy is certainly more in line with the law as it was generally thought to be before the decision in *Anderson*.

Conspiracy at common law

The only conspiracies left at common law are conspiracy to defraud, conspiracy to corrupt public morals and conspiracy to outrage public decency, although outraging public decency may well be a criminal offence in itself and therefore covered by section 1.

Conspiracy to defraud. A conspiracy to defraud was defined in *Scott* v. *Commissioner of Police* (1975) as;

> ". . . an agreement by two or more by dishonesty to deprive a person of something which is his or to which he is or would be or might be entitled, and an agreement by two or more by dishonesty to injure some proprietary right of his. . ."

Authority: *Scott* v. *Metropolitan Police Commissioner* (1975). D and others agreed to copy certain films without permission and without paying fees, and to make money by showing these films and charging for admission. There was no deception involved and therefore an offence under the Theft Act 1968 was difficult to prove. The House of Lords held that this was a conspiracy to defraud and deceit was unnecessary for that offence.

The elements of the offence were further clarified in *Moses and Ansbro*, where no economic loss was actually caused. This was held to be irrelevant.

Authority: *Moses and Ansbro* (1991). Ds, who were civil servants, had agreed a course of action which allowed immigrants to obtain National Insurance numbers and therefore gain work permits when they were not eligible. They were acting contrary to their public duty in so doing, and it was irrelevant that no actual financial loss had been caused.

Authority: *Wai Yu Tsang* (1992). The same point has been made most recently by the Privy Council. D had agreed with others not to enter certain dishonoured cheques on the records of the bank, in order to save the bank's reputation. It was held that the motive was irrelevant as was the fact that no loss was caused. He had imperilled the economic and proprietory interests of others by his agreement and actions. That was sufficient for liability.

Because of the unclear nature of the relevant sections of the Criminal Law Act there has been a considerable amount of case law on the overlap between section 1 conspiracy and conspiracy to defraud, and it was initially held that if there is an offence of conspiracy committed which is both a conspiracy to defraud and a conspiracy to commit a crime, the defendant should be charged under section 1 of the Criminal Law Act with statutory conspiracy and not with conspiracy to defraud.

Because of the confusion and uncertainty caused by this interpretation of the statute it was necessary for parliament to intervene and the law is now governed by section 12 of the Criminal Justice Act 1988 which amends section 5 of the Criminal Law Act 1977 to read;

"5(1) Subject to the following provisions of this section, the offence of conspiracy at common law is hereby abolished.

5(2) Subsection 1 above shall not affect the offence of conspiracy at common law so far as relates to conspiracy to defraud."

This means that where within a fact situation there is an overlap between conspiracy to commit a crime and conspiracy to defraud, the prosecution can choose which charge to bring.

Conspiracy to corrupt public morals

This offence first appeared in a modern case in 1963.

Authority: *Shaw* v. *Director of Public Prosecutions* (1963). D published a "Ladies Directory" containing details of prostitutes and was charged with conspiring with the prostitutes to corrupt public morals. The House of Lords held that there was such an offence at common law, and affirmed D's conviction.

Later cases restricted the application of the case.

Authority: *D.P.P.* v. *Withers* (1975). D and others had by deceit induced people to part with information which it was against their duty to disclose. The House of Lords rejected the suggestion that *Shaw* had created an offence of conspiracy to effect a public mischief, and held that no such offence existed.

Authority: *Knuller* v. *D.P.P.* (1973). D and others had published advertisements in a contact magazine aimed at male homosexuals. The House of Lords held that this was a conspiracy to corrupt public morals, thus confirming that this offence did exist. However, their Lordships did define the offence in very strong terms, thus limiting its application, and they rejected the idea put forward in *Shaw* that the House had a residual power to create new common law offences.

Conspiracy to outrage public decency. There is an offence at common law of outraging public decency, and therefore it is an offence to conspire to do so.

Authority: *Knuller* v. *D.P.P.* (See above.) This offence too was defined in very strong terms, and was said to go ". . . considerably beyond offending the susceptibilities of, or even shocking, reasonable people."

As the act, if carried out, amounts to a criminal offence, such a conspiracy would now be a statutory conspiracy under section 1.

It has recently been confirmed that outraging public decency is itself a substantive offence.

Authority: *Gibson* (1990). The defendant, an artist, had included in a public display of his work a pair of earrings made from freeze dried foetuses. He was convicted of the common law offence of outraging public decency.

Conspiracy to do the impossible

The law relating to impossible conspiracies is in line with the law of impossible attempts under the Criminal Attempts Act 1981.

The authority on impossible attempts, *Shivpuri*, (see below), can therefore be applied by analogy to impossible conspiracies.

For a discussion of the different types of impossibility see below, under Impossible Attempts.

ATTEMPTS

The law relating to liability for attempts is now governed by the Criminal Attempts Act 1981.

Criminal Attempts Act 1981

Proximity. Under section (1) of the Act;

> "If, with intent to commit an offence to which this section applies, a person does an act which is more than merely preparatory to the commission of the offence, he is guilty of attempting to commit the offence."

The question of whether an act is more than merely preparatory is a question of fact to be left to the jury. The judge must not usurp the jury's functions.

The common law tests of proximity, such as the "last act" test and the "equivocality" test, may be some help to a jury in deciding what kinds of act might be proximate enough to constitute attempt, although they have been superseded by the test in the Act.

It may be that the test under the Act; "acts which are more than merely preparatory," is even vaguer, but it is clear that attempts to be more specific have not been helpful, and given that it is a question of fact for the jury to decide, detailed explanation would be out of place.

Authority: *Gullefer* (1986). D tried to distract dogs in a greyhound race in order to get a call of "no race" and so retrieve his stake. He was charged with attempted theft. The case turned on whether what he had done was "more than merely preparatory" to the commission of the theft. At trial the Rubicon test—has the defendant "burnt his boats" and reached the point of no return—was referred to. On appeal this test was rejected. None of the specific pre-1981 tests apply. It is question of fact for the jury, based on the wording of the Act. *Conviction quashed —P. 312 Smith*

Mens rea for attempts. The *mens rea* of an attempt is set out in section 1(1) of the Act: "If *with intent* to commit an offence ..."

As with incitement and conspiracy, attempt is a crime of specific intent, and only intent will suffice. The Criminal Law Act has made no change in this respect.

This requirement does not however apply to the *mens rea* for the circumstances of an offence.

Authority: *Khan* (1990). The defendant was charged with attempted rape. He had attempted to have intercourse with a woman, being reckless as to whether or not she consented. He was found guilty and appealed on the basis that in order to be liable for attempt it should be proved that he knew or intended that she did not consent. The Court of Appeal held that section 1(1) of the 1981 Act required intent as to the act and any consequences only. The requisite *mens rea* for the circumstances relevant to the offence was the same as for the complete offence: in this case recklessness.

The situation with regard to consequences is more straightforward.

Authority: *Mohan* (1976). D refused to stop his car when signalled by a P.C. Instead he drove straight at the P.C. who managed to avoid him. He was charged with attempt to cause grievous bodily harm. His conviction was quashed because the jury had been misdirected regarding *mens rea* for attempt.

The Court of Appeal defined *mens rea* in these circumstances as:

> "a decision to bring about, insofar as it lies within the accused's power, the commission of the offence which it is alleged the accused attempted to commit, no matter whether the accused desired that consequence or not."

This excludes recklessness and foresight of probable or likely consequences. It looks very much like the concept of intention put forward in *Moloney*.

This is still the case, after the 1981 Act.

Authority: *Walker and Hayles* (1990). Ds had thrown their victim off a third floor balcony and seriously injured him. They were convicted of attempted murder and appealed on the basis that the meaning of intention in attempts was restricted to purpose or direct intent. The Court of Appeal, affirming their convictions, made it clear that intention has only one meaning. The cases on homicide are applicable to all cases of intent.

Attempting the impossible

Under section 1(2) of the Act:

> "A person may be guilty of attempting to commit an offence to which this section applies even though the facts are such that the commission of the offence is impossible."

Up until 1985, cases held that the Act had succeeded in making it an offence to attempt to do something which is a criminal offence but in the circumstances is either factually or legally totally impossible.

However, the first case to go to the House of Lords threw doubt upon the efficacy of the Act and liability for impossible attempts.

Authority: *Anderton* v. *Ryan* (1985). D was charged with attempt to dishonestly handle a video recorder. D had received it believing it to be stolen, but the police could not produce positive evidence that it was stolen and the case had to proceed on the basis that it was not.

The House of Lords held that no section of the Act made it an offence to attempt to do something which if the defendant had done all he intended to do, no crime would have been committed. That was the case here. Although section 1(3) may well have been intended to cover this type of situation, it did not on a literal interpretation do so.

Section 1 subsection (3) states:

"In any case where—
  (a) apart from this subsection a person's intention would not be regarded as having amounted to an intent to commit an offence; but
  (b) if the facts of the case had been as he believed them to be, his intention would be so regarded, then for the purposes of subsection (1) above he shall be regarded as having an intent to commit that offence."

The House of Lords held that the subsection did not cover the *Anderton* v. *Ryan* situation because lack of *mens rea* is not the problem. It is a lack of one element of the *actus reus*, the circumstances that the goods are stolen, which is missing. Section 1(3) was fairly obviously intended to cover this situation however and on a different basis of interpretation it could have been found to do so.

Shivpuri has now overruled *Anderton* v. *Ryan* and re-interpreted the Act. Lord Bridge, who gave one of the leading judgements in *Anderton* v. *Ryan* also gave judgement in *Shivpuri*, and the issues were re-assessed.

Authority: *Shivpuri* (1986). D was convicted of attempting to be knowingly concerned in dealing with a prohibited drug. He brought through customs what he thought was a prohibited drug, but was in fact a harmless substance. The House of Lords held that on the true construction of section 1(1) of the Criminal Attempts Act 1981 D was guilty, even if the facts were such that the actual offence was impossible of commission. Even though it was less than a year since the House of Lords gave judgement in the case, *Anderton* v. *Ryan* was overruled.

Lord Bridge said that considering the statute from first principles without taking into account *Anderton* v. *Ryan*, he now felt it was clear that all that was needed was an act more than merely preparatory to the commission of the offence D *intended* to commit. Such an act was present in this case, and his Lordship could find no clear distinguishing principle to differentiate *Anderton* v. *Ryan*. It was clear from the Law Commission's Report on Attempt and Impossibility that the *Anderton* v. *Ryan* fact situation was intended to be covered by the Act, and the House of Lords should have taken note of it in that case.

The judgement of the House of Lords in *Shivpuri* thus confirms the effectiveness of the Criminal Attempts Act. A defendant will be guilty of an attempt to commit a crime if he does an act which is more than merely preparatory towards that crime, even if the commission of the full offence is either factually or legally impossible for any reason.

Reforms

The Law Commission recommends only minor reforms to the law in this area. The Code would bring incitement, at present a common law offence, into line with the statutory offences of conspiracy and attempt, and thus iron out the few anomalies. (See, *e.g. Fitzmaurice*, above.) It would remain an offence to incite to attempt, and the offence of inciting to conspire would be re-introduced for the sake of uniformity.

Despite the long wait for changes in the law in relation to the remaining common law conspiracies, the Law Commission recommends no change. A separate report on conspiracy to defraud is expected.

The Code would also cancel out the effects, including the *obiter* statement, of the House of Lords decision in *Anderson*, above. Recklessness as to circumstances would be sufficient for liability for conspiracy and for attempt if it were enough for the complete offence, as in *Khan*.

The Law Commission also recommends that there be no exemption from liability for conspiracy for spouses, children or victims.

SUMMARY

The main topics for revision are:

Incitement

Mens rea of incitement
Inciting the impossible (*Fitzmaurice*)

Conspiracy

Statutory Conspiracy
Section 1(1), Criminal Law Act
Section 1(2), Criminal Law Act (*Anderson, Siracusa*)
Conspiracy at Common Law
Conspiracy to Defraud (*Scott* v. *M.P.C.*, *Moses and Ansbro*, Criminal Justice Act 1988)
Conspiracy to Corrupt Public Morals (*Shaw* v. *D.P.P.*, *D.P.P.* v. *Withers*, *Knuller* v. *D.P.P.*)
Conspiracy to Outrage Public Decency (*Knuller* v. *D.P.P.*, *Gibson*)
Conspiracy to do the Impossible (Criminal Attempts Act, *Shivpuri*)

Attempts

Criminal Attempts Act 1981
Proximity (section 1(1), Criminal Attempts Act, *Gullefer*)
Mens Rea for Attempts (section 1(1), Criminal Attempts Act)
(*Khan, Mohan, Walker and Hayles*)
Attempting the Impossible

(Section 1(2), Criminal Attempts Act)
(*Anderton* v. *Ryan*, section 1(3), *Shivpuri*)

Reforms
Draft Criminal Code

---

6. GENERAL DEFENCES

As well as specific defences to particular crimes, there exist a number of defences available to all crimes.

The main general defences are as follows:
Insanity, automatism, self-defence, and duress. Although there is no general defence of necessity available in English law, the topic is usually considered in most syllabuses at this stage. Similarly, intoxication and mistake, while not amounting to general defences, in some circumstances reduce or excuse liability and are therefore dealt with in this chapter.

These defences are called "general" because the judges have made them available to crimes generally, in contrast with specific defences to individual offences formulated by Parliament.

Only insanity has to be proved (on a balance of probabilities): with the others, D is entitled to the benefit of the doubt and the burden of proof is on the prosecution.

INSANITY

The defence of insanity has been developed by case law. The basic legal definition stems from an 1843 case and problems have arisen as the definition has not been developed to take account of medical and legal progress.

The case in point is the trial for murder of Daniel M'naghten who was acquitted on the ground of insanity. Questions were put by the judges to the House of Lords in order to clarify the legal rules on the defence, and the answers to those questions became the M'naghten Rules.

Authority: *M'naghten Rules* (1843).
The Rules state that every man is presumed to be sane until the contrary is proved, and that to establish insanity:

> ". . . it must be clearly proved that at the time of the committing of the act the party accused was labouring under such a defect of reason, from disease of the mind, as not to know the nature and quality of the act he was doing; or, if he did know it, that he did not know he was doing what was wrong."

The burden is therefore to show, on a balance of probabilities, that the defendant is insane. This leads to a verdict of not guilty by reason of insanity. However, defendants rarely raise this plea as the automatic committal to a mental institution for an indefinite period is usually a much harsher sentence than any he would get if found guilty of an offence.

Disease of the mind

"Disease of the mind" has been considered in several cases. The legal definition does not necessarily coincide with the medical definition.

Authority: *Kemp* (1957). D attacked his wife with a hammer causing her grievous bodily harm. He was suffering from arteriosclerosis which caused him to have temporary blackouts.

Disease of the mind was defined in this case. "Mind" covers the ordinary mental faculties of reason, memory and understanding, and does not mean the brain in the physical sense. A disease of the mind can be temporary or permanent, curable or incurable.

Later cases have developed the definition further to cover a range of illnesses which neither in medical nor everyday language would be classed as insanity.

Authority: *Attorney General for Northern Ireland* v. *Bratty* (1963). D killed a girl during a mental blackout said to be due to psychomotor epilepsy. Lord Denning said, *obiter*, that a mental disease is a disease of the mind if it manifests itself in violence and is prone to recur. Subsequent cases have confined this very wide definition somewhat.

Authority: *Quick* (1973). D, a diabetic, injured a person while suffering from hypoglycaemia. The trial judge ruled that, having raised his state of mind as an issue in pleading automatism, D's only possible defence was insanity. D then pleaded guilty and appealed against the ruling. The Court of Appeal allowed the appeal and held that the blackout was caused by alcohol and lack of food combined with insulin, and not by the disease itself. External factors causing a mental disorder will not be classed as a disease of the mind. The same point is made in *Bailey* (below).

This does not mean that diabetes can never be classed as a disease of the mind for the purposes of legal insanity. A recent case has illustrated that the situation is rather more complicated than that.

Authority: *Hennessey* (1989). D was charged with taking a conveyance without authority and driving while disqualified. He was a diabetic who had been suffering from stress, and the stress had affected his blood sugar level and his requirement of insulin. His dose had therefore been inadequate and he had been suffering from hyperglycaemia. He pleaded automatism and the judge raised the question of insanity. D changed his plea to guilty and appealed against conviction. On appeal the Court of Appeal said that the important question was whether this was a disease of the mind within *M'naghten*, and that depended on whether it was caused by internal or external factors. They held that hyperglycaemia was an inherent factor caused by the diabetes. The stress and anxiety could not be treated as external causative factors.

Quick was distinguished because hypoglycaemia is caused by external factors such as alcohol, food or too much insulin, and not by the diabetes itself. The Court justified this on the basis that the distinction is meant to protect the public against the recurrence of dangerous conduct which is difficult to control, but it is difficult to see why too little insulin cannot be an external factor just as too much would be, or what purpose is to be served by potentially committing diabetics to an indefinite period in a secure mental hospital. Nevertheless the distinction is crucial.

Authority: *Bingham* (1991). D was a diabetic who was charged with theft, and who claimed he was hypoglycaemic at the time of the offences. His conviction was quashed by the Court of Appeal because the trial judge did not correctly distinguish between hypo- and hyper-glycaemia.

A similar anomalous result was achieved in respect of epilepsy in an earlier House of Lords case.

Authority: *Sullivan* (1983). D had kicked and injured a man during an attack of psychomotor epilepsy. Medical evidence stated that this probably happened unknown to the accused during the third stage of an attack. The judge said he would have to direct the jury on insanity and D changed his plea to guilty and then appealed against conviction. The House of Lords held that epilepsy was a disease of the mind because D's mental faculties were impaired to the extent of causing a defect of reason. It was irrelevant that this was an organic disease which was only intermittent. It would also be irrelevant if it were only temporary.

Sleepwalking had previously been thought to be an example of automatism rather than insanity, but it is now clear that the courts will treat sleepwalking as an example of disease of the mind with internal causes unless there is clear evidence of an external causal factor.

Authority: *Burgess* (1991). D committed an offence of violence while sleepwalking. The Court of Appeal held that the sleepwalking was caused by an internal factor, and that the ordinary stresses and anxieties of life which may have brought about the sleepwalking were not sufficient to constitute an external factor.

Defect of reason

Once a disease of the mind is established it must be proved that it caused a defect of reason which had one of two consequences: *either* the defendant did not know the nature and quality of his act, *or* he did not know his act was wrong.

A defect of reason must be more than just a lapse of normal reasoning power in a stressful situation.

Authority: *Clarke* (1972). D was accused of theft from a shop. Her defence rested on forgetfulnes due to depression. The trial judge held that this raised the issue of insanity and she changed her plea to guilty and then appealed. The Court of Appeal quashed her conviction saying that defect of reason implied a loss of reasoning power and not a mere temporary lapse due to forgetfulness.

Nature and quality of the Act. This covers the rare situation where the defendant, because of a defect of reason, does not understand the physical nature and quality of his act.

Delusions as to the moral nature of his act do not excuse a defendant.

Knowledge that the Act was wrong. This has been held to mean legally, rather than morally, wrong.

Authority: *Windle* (1952). D killed his wife by an overdose of aspirin. Medical evidence was given that although he was suffering from a mental illness he knew that what he was doing was legally wrong. The Court of Appeal affirmed his conviction on the basis that the court cannot and should not make decisions as to moral rights and wrongs and can only decide what is contrary to law.

Court procedure

If the defendant puts his mental state in issue, *e.g.* by raising a defence of automatism or diminished responsibility, then the prosecution can raise the issue of insanity and bring evidence to prove it.

Proposals for reform

The M'naghten Rules are almost universally regarded as unsatisfactory, and reforms have been periodically suggested. The most recent are those set out in the Law Commission's Draft Criminal Code, which adopts the recommendations of the Butler Committee, with some amendments. A jury would be able to return a verdict of not guilty on evidence of mental disorder, and the courts would have flexible disposal powers in responding to such a verdict. The verdict would be available either if all the act and fault elements of an offence were present but there was evidence of a severe mental illness or handicap which was relevant to the commission of the offence, or where fault could not be proved because of mental disorder.

A verdict of manslaughter by reason of diminished responsibility can be returned by a jury instead of murder, in certain circumstances (see Chap. 8). This has allowed defendants in a wide variety of circumstances involving mental impairment or disease, an alternative to the insanity defence.

AUTOMATISM

Automatism applies to the rare situation where the defendant is not legally insane but for some reason he is unable to control what he is doing, and none of the other general defences apply. It can be explained either in terms of a lack of *actus reus*, as the act is not voluntary, or a lack of *mens rea*, because the defendant is not conscious of what he is doing.

This inability to control one's acts must result from some external factor and not from a disease of the mind constituting insanity. Automatism may occur for example when a defendant is in concussion, in a hypoglycaemic episode or in a hypnotic trance, provided that there is an external and not an internal cause.

The external factor could be a traumatic event inducing severe shock, although it must be something which results in more than general stress and anxiety, as in *Hennessey*, or *Burgess*. A good example is post-traumatic stress disorder, now increasingly recognised by the courts.

Authority: *T.* (1990). A few days after having been raped, D was involved in an incident which led to charges of robbery and causing actual bodily harm. Medical evidence showed that she was suffering from post-traumatic stress disorder and was not aware of what was happening. The court held that her state of mind was caused by the external event of the rape, and was therefore classed as automatism.

Authority: *Quick* (see above). D's conviction was quashed because the judge had ruled evidence of automatism inadmissible. The Court of Appeal said that such a situation could give rise to a defence of automatism.

Self-induced automatism

Self-induced automatism can operate to negative the *mens rea* of *any* offence provided it is not caused by drink or drugs to which different rules apply for policy reasons.

Authority: *Bailey* (1983). D, a diabetic, attacked his ex-girlfriend's new boyfriend and injured him. He had felt unwell beforehand and had taken some sugar but no food. He suffered a hypoglycaemic episode during which he committed the assault. At trial the judge refused to allow evidence of automatism as his state was self-induced.

On appeal the Court of Appeal held that self-induced automatism other than that caused by drink or drugs can negative the *mens rea* of an offence, provided that the accused's conduct in the light of his knowledge of the likely results of his acts or omissions does not amount to recklessness.

This case keeps automatism per se out of the difficult policy area of intoxication unless drink or drugs are involved, but it does present similar problems of coincidence of *actus reus* and *mens rea* (see below).

Automatism and insanity—a comparison

A verdict of not guilty due to automatism leads to an acquittal.

A verdict of not guilty due to insanity leads to indefinite detention in a secure mental hospital.

If a lack of voluntary behaviour is due to an outside factor, such as medication, a blow on the head or a traumatic event, a defence of automatism can succeed (*Quick*, *T.*), even if the automatism is self-induced (*Bailey*).

If a lack of voluntary behaviour is due to an inherent mental condition or illness, this can be a disease of the mind (*Sullivan*, *Burgess*), even if the illness or condition is temporary and curable.

If a lack of voluntary behaviour is caused by drink or drugs then the specific rules relating to intoxication will apply (see below).

MISTAKE

Mistake is not strictly speaking a defence, but a mistake or accident can negate liability if its effect is to negate the necessary *mens rea*. Although not a defence in the true sense, it is often dealt with, and overlaps with, other defences.

Intention or *Cunningham* recklessness

If the *mens rea* required is either intention or *Cunningham* recklessness, (see Chap. 2), then any mistake which means that the defendant did not either intend an element of the *actus reus* or did not subjectively realise the risk involved, will be one which negatives *mens rea*. For example, if one element of the offence is lack of consent, and the requisite *mens rea* in relation to that element is subjective recklessness, as in rape, then an honest mistake will negative *mens rea*, however unreasonable it is.

Authority: *Morgan* (1976). D and friends had been drinking. D encouraged his friends to have sexual intercourse with his wife saying that she would protest but would not mean it. They did so and ignored her protests. They pleaded not guilty to rape because they had believed that she had consented. On appeal against conviction the House of Lords said that an honest, albeit unreasonable, belief in the victim's consent would be enough to negate liability as *mens rea* would be missing. However they applied the proviso in this case and the convictions were therefore affirmed. The Sexual Offences (Amendment) Act 1976 confirmed this rule in relation to rape.

Caldwell recklessness

According to *Caldwell* a person is reckless if he does not give any thought to a risk when a reasonable person would have realised the risk.

Where a person is reckless in the *Caldwell* sense by not having adverted to the risk at all, it is difficult to see how there could be a question of mistake. In order to make a mistake concerning an element of *actus reus* it must surely be necessary to give some thought to it, as in the *Morgan* situation.

Negligence

If an offence requires only negligence with regard to an element of the *actus reus* then *ex hypothesi*, only a mistake which is reasonable will negative the negligence.

Strict liability

If no *mens rea* is required with regard to one element of the *actus reus* then even an honest and reasonable mistake with regard to that element will not negative liability.

Mistake as to an element of a defence

There are some statutory crimes where a defence is defined in terms of reasonableness. In such a case any mistake relevant to the validity of such a defence must obviously be reasonable.

Mistake as to an element of actus reus

Just as with lack of consent (see *Morgan*, above), many offences against the person require unlawfulness as one of the circumstances of the *actus reus*. Lack of unlawfulness because of a mistake can negative this.

Authority: *Kimber* (1983). D was charged with indecent assault. He said he had believed that his victim had consented but no evidence was given as to the reasonableness of that belief. He was convicted and appealed. The Court of Appeal held that the lack of consent, which would make the act unlawful, was an element of the offence and the prosecution had to prove the necessary *mens rea*. If the defendant honestly believed that the victim consented, one element of the offence, the unlawfulness, would be missing and the defendant would not be guilty.

The same approach is now taken with regard to defence of self or another. Although previously in *Albert* v. *Lavin* (1982), it had been held that a belief in a right to self-defence must be reasonable in any given situation, this is no longer the case. The reasoning in *Kimber* applies to any defence which is related to the lawfulness of the defendant's actions, whether it be consent, self-defence, defence of another or prevention of crime.

Authority: *Gladstone Williams* (1983). D mistook his victim for a mugger attacking a youth and fought him off. His victim had falsely claimed to be a policeman but was in fact a passer-by trying to arrest the youth who had attacked and robbed a woman. D was charged with assault occasioning actual bodily harm. He claimed that he honestly believed his victim was assaulting the youth and that he was entitled to prevent the crime occurring. On appeal his conviction was quashed: the prosecution had to disprove the possibility that the defendant had made an honest mistake of fact. If a belief was honestly held its unreasonableness was irrelevant.

This approach has been confirmed by the Privy Council.

Authority: *Beckford* (1987). D was a policeman who had shot and killed a suspect. His defence was that he had mistakenly believed his victim was about to shoot him. The trial court held that such a belief must be reasonably held in order to exculpate, but the Privy Council on appeal held that the circumstances must be taken to be as the defendant saw them, whether or not that was a reasonable interpretation of them. The defendant therefore had a defence of self-defence, because the killing was not unlawful if, in the circumstances as he perceived them to be, he had used reasonable force to defend himself. Although this in one sense confuses the distinction between elements of the *actus reus* and defences, it does clarify the situation in respect of mistake.

However, it is important to remember that in relation to self-defence and the prevention of crime there is still a requirement of reasonableness as regards the amount of force used (see below). A person may make an *unreasonable* mistake as to when he can defend himself and not be guilty of an offence, but he can only make a *reasonable* mistake as to how much force he may use to do so.

It is therefore now settled law that an honest but unreasonable belief as to a factor relating to the unlawfulness of one's conduct is sufficient to negative *mens rea*.

Mistake of law

There is a general rule that ignorance of the criminal law is no defence, even if the ignorance is reasonable in the circumstances.

Mistakes which must be reasonable

There are now very few offences where a mistake must be reasonable as well as honest. The main ones are;
  (a) Crimes of negligence.
  (b) Statutory crimes where a defence is defined in terms of reasonableness.

Reforms

The Draft Criminal Code makes the following recommendation in respect of mistake; if a person believes in the existence of circumstances, he will have any defence he would have had if the circumstances had been as he thought. This applies a subjective test to all mistakes as to circumstances, and is in line with the recommendation as to the subjective nature of recklessness.

CONSENT

Consent, as with mistake, is not a true defence. If a victim "consents" then the act is not normally unlawful, and therefore part of the *actus reus* is missing. Nevertheless, the Court of Appeal has recently treated consent as a defence sometimes but not always applicable to non-fatal offences against the person.

Authority: *Brown* (1991). Ds were involved in a series of sado-masochistic sexual acts in private. They all consented. Injuries were caused to some of the participants. They were convicted of offences under sections 47 and 20 of the Offences Against the Person Act 1861, and appealed against conviction on the grounds that the victims' consent negated the unlawfulness of their actions. The Court of Appeal held that all actions causing bodily harm will be assaults, and a prima facie defence of consent may sometimes but not always be available. In this case it is not available because the harm caused is more than merely transient and there was "no good reason" for causing it. The approach in the case wavers between treating consent as an *actus reus* issue and a defence issue, in the same way as occurs in the self-defence cases (see below). Leave to appeal to the House of Lords has been granted.

INTOXICATION

In some circumstances the defendant may not have the *mens rea* at the time he commits the *actus reus* because he is so intoxicated with alcohol or other drugs that he does not know what he is doing. Technically speaking this lack of *mens rea* should lead to an acquittal but strong policy reasons against this have led the courts to evolve a way of dealing with such cases which will normally lead to a conviction.

Voluntary intoxication is not strictly speaking a defence. However, it can negative *specific intent*, but even then it may be shown that the intoxication did not prevent the defendant from having the necessary intent required for the crime, and he will still be liable. In crimes of basic intent the *mens rea* is assumed, and need not be proven.

Authority: *D.P.P.* v. *Majewski* (1976). D was involved in a fight while suffering from the effect of alcohol and drugs and unaware of what he was doing. The House of Lords held that evidence of voluntary intoxication cannot negative *mens rea* in a crime of basic intent. Although he was not aware of what he was doing, D could not be said to be acting involuntarily in the ordinary sense of the word, and therefore he had the necessary basic intent.

Section 8 of the Criminal Justice Act 1967 which says that an accused must not be taken as a matter of law to have intended the natural and probable consequences of his acts simply because they were natural and probable, has no application here. *Majewski* is based very firmly on policy and is difficult to explain in logical legal terms.

People who voluntarily take alcohol or drugs should realise the possible consequences in terms of violent behaviour and uncontrollable actions. They can therefore be said to be *Caldwell* reckless in taking such a risk. However, when the drug taken normally has a soporific effect the defendant cannot be said to be reckless as to the possible consequence if it has a totally unpredictable effect on him.

Authority: *Hardie* (1984). D quarrelled with the woman he was living with and took some of her valium tablets to calm himself down. While under the influence of the drugs he set fire to the flat. His defence to a charge of criminal damage with intent to endanger life or being reckless as to endangering life was that he lacked *mens rea* due to the drug's effect. On appeal against conviction the Court of Appeal held that the usual rules regarding intoxication as a defence did not apply where the normal effect of the drug was soporific, and it should have been left to the jury to consider whether the defendant was reckless.

Crimes of basic and specific intent

The distinction between crimes of basic intent and crimes of specific intent is discussed earlier (see Chap. 2), and is particularly relevant to intoxication.

Mens rea for crimes of basic intent can be either recklessness or intention.

Mens rea for crimes of specific intent is intention, nothing less sufficing.

The distinction is not an entirely logical one, however, and a list of crimes and their categories based on particular cases is the safest way to distinguish them.

Voluntary intoxication for Dutch Courage

If the defendant deliberately gets himself intoxicated in order to give himself the courage to commit an offence, which he subsequently commits when so intoxicated that it might be hard to prove he had the *mens rea* at that time, he will be unable to claim lack of intent, even in respect of a crime of specific intent.

Authority: *Attorney General for Northern Ireland* v. *Gallagher* (1961). D decided to kill his wife. He brought a knife and a bottle of whisky which he drank to give himself Dutch courage. Then he killed her with the knife. The House of Lords held that he was guilty of murder and could not claim to have lacked intent or been insane.

Intoxication and defences

The Court of Appeal has considered the question of the relevance of intoxication when a defendant was relying on a defence of self-defence. Given the subjective approach to this as evidenced by *Beckford*, the approach to intoxication could make a difference to liability. The Court of Appeal rejected the relevance of the distinction between crimes of basic and specific intent when it came to defences, and said that a mistake arising from voluntary intoxication could never be relied on in putting forward a defence, whatever the crime. This was a novel extension of the rules relating to voluntary intoxication.

Authority: *O'Grady* (1987). D, because of intoxication, mistakenly thought he was being attacked by a friend and reacted violently, causing death. D was convicted of manslaughter and appealed against conviction,

relying on the defence of self-defence in the circumstances as he mistakenly believed them to be. The Court dismissed the appeal for the
reasons explained above.

This case evoked considerable criticism for its approach. It was reconsidered by the Court of Appeal recently, and its decision highlighted the
inconsistency of the earlier case.

Authority: *O'Connor* (1991). D while drunk head-butted his victim,
who died. D claimed he thought he was acting in self-defence. He was
convicted of murder and appealed on the grounds that his mistaken belief
was relevant. The Court of Appeal held that whereas, following *O'Grady*,
there was no need to mention the intoxicated mistake in respect of the
defence of self-defence, it should have been mentioned in the context of
proving the specific intent necessary for murder. His conviction was
quashed and a manslaughter conviction substituted. It was clear from
Beckford and from *O'Grady* that the same issue could be looked at alternatively as either a question of *mens rea* as to unlawfulness or the defence of
self-defence. It is unacceptable that a different result can be reached on
the same facts, depending on which approach is taken.

Authority: *Jaggard* v. *Dickinson* (1981). D broke into a house which she
thought belonged to a friend of hers who had given her permission to treat
the house as her own. That mistake, though caused by voluntary intoxication was enough to exculpate the defendant, by allowing her to rely on the
statutory defence of lawful excuse under section 5(2) of the Criminal
Damage Act. Because the test is specifically set out in subjective terms,
the Court held that the reasons for a subjective belief in lawful excuse were
irrelevant, and the defendant was acquitted. This case is relevant only to
the specific defence of lawful excuse under the Act, and has no wider
application.

PRIVATE DEFENCE

This term covers defence of oneself and others, defence of one's property,
preventing crime and assisting lawful arrest.

The defendant has a defence if he uses necessary and reasonable force in
any of the above situations. This is controlled partly by common law and
partly by section 3(1) of the Criminal Law Act 1967.

Authority: *Beckford* (1987). (See above.)

If the defendant makes a mistake as to his right to self-defence because
he is voluntarily intoxicated however, the circumstances will not be
viewed through his eyes, but through the eyes of a sober person, as the
mistake will not be admissible in evidence. (See *O'Grady*, *O'Connor*,
above.)

Reasonable force

A person can only use such force as is reasonable in all the circumstances, and it is up to the jury to decide whether it was, as it is a question of fact not law.

Authority: *Bird* (1985). D had been slapped and pushed by a man. She was holding a glass in her hand at the time and she had hit out at the man in self defence without realising that she still held the glass. The trial judge directed the jury that self-defence was only available as a defence if the defendant had first shown an unwillingness to fight. The Court of Appeal quashed D's conviction saying that it was unnecessary to show an unwillingness to fight and there were circumstances where D might reasonably react immediately and without first retreating. It was up to a jury to decide on the facts of the case.

Pre-emptive self-defence

It is not absolutely necessary that the defendant be attacked first. In some circumstances he may act pre-emptively to prevent an attack.

Authority: *Attorney General's Reference No. 2 of 1983.* An individual can protect himself in advance from attack, for example by arming himself or making a bomb, and this can constitute self-defence.

Excessive force

The use of excessive force indicates that the defendant has acted unreasonably in the circumstances. There will therefore be no valid defence, and the defendant will be liable for the crime.

This may seem rather harsh in some circumstances, particularly on a murder charge. If a defendant acts under provocation, for example, and kills someone intentionally, a charge of murder is reduced to manslaughter (see Chap. 7). There is no similar rule with regard to excessive use of force in self-defence even though there may be a considerable overlap between the two situations.

Authority: *McInnes* (1971). D was involved in a fight between two rival gangs. He had a knife and he claimed that his victim ran on to it. He appealed against conviction saying that the judge's direction on excessive self-defence was wrong in law.

The Court of Appeal held that there was no provision for murder to be reduced to manslaughter in such circumstances but a defendant cannot be expected to act coolly and calmly in this kind of situation or measure his response accurately. A jury must take into account the fact that the defendant acted on the spur of the moment under stress, and if they felt that he acted honestly then this would be strong evidence of reasonableness. The Court also pointed out the possibility of provocation as an alternative defence.

The effect of this approach towards reasonableness is in practice more favourable to the accused than an alternative verdict of manslaughter would be, as it will almost certainly lead to an acquittal where a verdict of manslaughter would be brought in if it were available.

Reasonableness in self-defence: conclusion

If a defendant makes an honest but unreasonable mistake as to whether he has a right to defend himself then he lacks *mens rea* as to the "unlawfulness" element and will not be guilty of an offence.

If a defendant makes an honest but unreasonable mistake as to the *degree* of force he can use, strictly speaking this is excessive self-defence and he will still be guilty of an offence.

Given the judgments in *Palmer* and *McInnes*, re-emphasised in later cases, a jury will be told that an honest belief regarding the amount of force necessary will be strong evidence of a reasonable belief and the likely outcome is that the defendant will be found not guilty.

DURESS BY THREATS

Duress covers the situation where the defendant is being forced by someone else to break the law under threat of serious harm befalling himself or someone else.

Duress is a defence to any crime except murder. The general reasoning behind its admissibility is that the criminal law should set a standard of behaviour for the reasonable man which does not require unreasonable powers of resistance.

Duress as a defence to murder

Duress is no longer available as a defence to a charge of murder, whether as a principal or secondary party, or to attempted murder.

Authority: *Howe* (1986). D and another were involved in one murder as secondary parties; they were also principals to another murder and had conspired to kill a third person. They put forward duress as a defence. They were convicted of murder as principals and appealed. The Court of Appeal held that duress by threats of immediate injury or death was no answer to a charge of murder unless the charge was one of secondary participation only, following the previous authority of *D.P.P.* v. *Lynch* (1975), which had held that duress was available as a defence to secondary participants in murder.

The Court admitted that the distinction between different kinds of participation in murder was illogical but said this did not necessarily mean that duress should be made available as a defence to the killer rather than withdrawing it as a defence for the secondary participant. Leave to appeal to the House of Lords was granted, and although the appeal was in respect of duress as a defence to murder as a principal, the House of Lords did take the opportunity to review the law thoroughly. They decided that the distinction between murder as a principal and murder as a secondary participant was illogical and should no longer exist. Duress should either be a defence to murder generally or no defence at all, and they chose the latter course. The decision has been much criticised, but despite some anomalies in the judgment and the fact that the appeal was about murder as a principal, the case is now generally taken to have overruled *D.P.P.* v. *Lynch* and changed the law.

Authority: *Gotts* (1992). D attempted to murder his mother. His father had threatened to shoot him unless he did so. His appeal against conviction on the grounds of duress failed. The House of Lords held that the same reasoning applied to attempted murder as to murder, and for similar reasons to those set out in *Howe*, the defence should not be applicable here. The intent to kill was obviously considered a sufficiently serious factor to justify denying the defence. The existence of such threats would however be a mitigating factor when it came to sentence, which cannot be the case in a murder conviction. There is an additional difficulty here in that if an alternative charge of wounding with intent under section 18 of the Offences Against the Person Act 1861 was preferred, the defence of duress would be available, and would lead to a complete acquittal.

Seriousness of the threats

Whether the threats will constitute a valid defence will depend on their seriousness and the seriousness of the crime. The defendant is expected to act as a reasonable man in his circumstances would do and the jury will decide on that basis whether the threats are serious enough.

Authority: *Graham* (1982). D was a homosexual who lived with his wife and his lover. He took part in the killing of his wife under threats from his lover and unsuccessfully raised the defence of duress. On appeal the Court of Appeal said that the trial judge had been correct in saying that the jury must decide not only whether D was in fear of his safety, but also that a reasonable man in such circumstances would have been. This was confirmed by the House of Lords in *Howe*, which held that the direction given by the Lord Chief Justice in *Graham* represented the correct law.

Threats to property will probably be insufficiently serious, even if much more serious than the crime the defendant is forced to commit. There is no recent case on the point.

Immediacy of the threat

The defence is unavailable to someone who could have taken alternative action to avoid the threat but did not do so. However, this restriction is generally interpreted in the defendant's favour.

Authority: *Hudson and Taylor* (1971). Ds said they had committed perjury under threat of injury and they felt that asking for police protection in court would not have helped them. The Court of Appeal said that the defence of duress should still have been left to the jury.

Voluntary membership of a gang

Recent cases have considered the situation where a defendant voluntarily becomes involved in a gang knowing that crimes may be committed, and then wishes to rely on the defence of duress to exculpate him from liability for those crimes.

Authority: *Sharp* (1987). D was charged with manslaughter, and pleaded duress due to threats from the rest of his gang if he did not take part in the killing. He was convicted and appealed. The Court of Appeal held that the defence was not available if he had voluntarily joined the gang and was aware at that time of the pressure which might be brought to bear on him. His conviction was upheld.

Authority: *Shepherd* (1987). D took part in a series of burglaries as part of a gang. He claimed that he did not necessarily know simply by joining the gang that he might be submitted to threats of violence to force him to take part in criminal activities. The judge withdrew the defence of duress from the jury and D was convicted. On appeal his conviction was quashed. The Court held that it was up to the jury to decide whether D had known of the possible pressures when he joined the gang, and the defence should have been left to the jury.

DURESS OF CIRCUMSTANCES

The defence of duress had always been thought to be limited to threats from another. Any other kind of pressure forcing someone to commit a crime was seen as necessity, a defence not generally thought to be available in English law. Recently, however, the Court of Appeal has blurred the distinction between duress and necessity, and a group of cases have been decided which refer to a kind of duress called duress of circumstances which looks very like a limited defence of necessity.

Authority: *Willer* (1987). D was charged with reckless driving. He had driven onto a pavement to escape from a gang of youths who were trying to attack his car and drag him out. He pleaded necessity, but the trial judge refused to let the defence go to the jury. On appeal his conviction was quashed. The Court indicated that a defence of duress should have been put to the jury. There were threats of violence to him unless he committed the crime, and therefore the case takes the defence of duress further than it has yet been taken. It looks very like necessity under another name.

Authority: *Martin* (1989). In the latest Court of Appeal case on this topic the defendant had been charged with driving while disqualified. He claimed that his wife had threatened to commit suicide if he did not drive their son to work, and that in the circumstances it was reasonable to take her seriously. The Court of Appeal held that English law did recognise a defence in these circumstances. They also referred to it as duress of circumstances. The defence applied if the defendant's reaction was reasonable and proportionate to avoid death or serious injury. It should be left to a jury to decide whether the defendant acted as he did because in the circumstances as he reasonably perceived them to be he had good cause to fear that death or serious injury might occur. If so he would have a defence if a reasonable man with his characteristics would have reacted in the same way. This brings the defence of duress of circumstances in line with duress by threats.

NECESSITY

Necessity has traditionally covered the situation where the defendant is faced with a choice of two evils but in this case the alternative evil is not a threat from another person but some other happening or circumstance.

English law does not recognise a general defence of necessity. Judicial opinion was that once the door was opened to such a defence it would be an excuse for all kinds of lawless behaviour. Nevertheless it does seem clear from the above cases that the door has been opened to a limited extent, and that we do have a limited defence of necessity by analogy with duress, whatever we may choose to call it.

In the wider situations not covered by duress of circumstances, the position at the moment seems to be that in genuine cases we should rely on police discretion not to prosecute. This attitude seems illogical and unsatisfactory but the leading case illustrates the possible problems which could arise in defining a defence of necessity.

Authority: *Dudley and Stephens* (1884). Ds, after being shipwrecked and without food and water for several days, killed and ate a third member of their crew. They were convicted of murder but the death sentence was eventually commuted to six months' imprisonment. The judgments vary in their reasoning, but it is generally accepted that the *ratio* denies any defence of necessity to murder.

There are moral and practical reasons for this, and it is of course in line with the present law relating to duress, but it is doubtful now that *Dudley and Stephens* has the wide and general effect previously attributed to it.

There are many offences specifically incorporating "unlawfully" or "without lawful authority or reasonable excuse" such as the Offences Against the Person Act 1861, the effect of which is to allow a necessity defence.

PROPOSALS FOR REFORM

The Law Commission's Consultation Paper No. 122, published in March 1992, updates the Draft Criminal Code's recommendations for reform of the general defences.

Intoxication

In contrast to the D.C.C. the Consultation Paper recommends that a major review of the law in this area be carried out, and that in the meantime the prevailing common law should be applied. The Consultation Paper points out that English case law on this topic has been rejected by other jurisdictions, and their reasoning should be considered before any changes are effected. The draft Bill merely sets out the law as it is at present.

Private and Public defence

Clause 28 of the Bill links private and public defence, listing the instances where use of force will come within either of those heads. It will be permissible to use an amount of force which is reasonable in the circumstances as D believes them to be, D will not be able to rely on any circumstances he is not aware of in order to justify his use of force.

Duress by threats

Clause 26 if enacted, would bring about major changes in this defence. The defence of duress by threats would be available to all offences, including murder and attempted murder, thus rejecting arguments in the recent detailed judgments of the House of Lords in those areas. Additionally, the test applied would be rather more subjective than the present test of whether a person of reasonable firmness would have reacted to the threats in the same way. The test will be rather whether this particular person could reasonably have been expected to resist the threats. The subject-matter of the threats will not be limited to D himself or close family.

Duress of circumstances

Provision for this defence is similar to that for duress by threats, reflecting the close analogy between the two.

Necessity

The Consultation Paper recognises some kinds of case which do not easily fit into either of the above categories, and would be better classed as cases of necessity. It gives as an example *In Re F.* (1990), involving medical treatment given to a person without consent in circumstances where they are unable to consent. Clause 31(3)(b) of the Bill therefore specifically saves any existing common law defence of necessity.

SUMMARY

The main topics for revision are:

Insanity

M'naghten Rules
Disease of the Mind (*Kemp*, *Bratty*, *Quick*, *Hennessey*, *Bingham*, *Sullivan*, *Burgess*)
Defect of Reason (*Clarke*)

Nature and Quality of the Act
Knowledge that the Act was Wrong (*Windle*)
Court Procedure
Reforms (Draft Criminal Code)

Automatism
(*T.*, *Quick*)
Self-induced Automatism (*Bailey*)
Automatism and Insanity: a Comparison

Mistake
Intention/*Cunningham* Recklessness (*Morgan*)
Caldwell Recklessness
Negligence
Strict Liability
Mistake as to an Element of a Defence
Mistake as to an Element of *Actus Reus* (*Kimber*, *Gladstone Williams*, *Beckford*)
Mistake of Law
Mistakes which must be Reasonable
Reforms (Draft Criminal Code)

Consent
(*Brown*)

Intoxication
(*Majewski*)
(*Hardie*)
Basic and Specific Intent and Intoxication
Voluntary Intoxication for Dutch Courage (*Gallagher*)
Intoxication and Defences (*O'Grady*, *O'Connor*, *Jaggard* v. *Dickinson*)

Private defence
The right to self-defence (*Beckford*)
Reasonable Force (*Bird*)
Pre-emptive Self Defence (*A.G.'s Reference No. 2 of 1983*)
Excessive Force (*McInnes*)
Reasonableness in Self-Defence

Duress by threats
Duress as a Defence to Murder and attempted murder (*Howe*, *Gotts*)
Seriousness of the Threat (*Graham*)
Immediacy of the Threat (*Hudson and Taylor*)
Voluntary membership of a gang (*Sharp*, *Shepherd*)

Duress of circumstances
(*Willer*, *Martin*)

Necessity
(*Dudley and Stephens*)

Reform proposals
Law Commission Consultation Paper No. 122
(Intoxication, Private and Public defence, Duress by threats, Duress of circumstances, Necessity)

---

7. NON-FATAL VIOLENCE OFFENCES

The main non-fatal violence offences, other than sexual offences, are common law assault and battery and the aggravated assault offences under the Offences Against the Person Act 1861, ss. 47, 20, and 18. Reform of this area of the law is the subject of the Law Commission Consultation Paper No. 122 published in March 1992.

ASSAULT AND BATTERY

In criminal law, as in civil law, assault and battery theoretically mean different things.

However, the two are almost always treated as one, as they were in *Kimber* (1983):

> "An assault is an act by which the defendant intentionally or recklessly causes the complainant to apprehend immediate, or to sustain, unlawful personal violence."

Assault and battery are now statutory offences covered by section 39 of the Criminal Justice Act 1988.

Actus reus of assault
The *actus reus* of assault is any act which causes the victim to apprehend an immediate infliction of violence such as raising a fist or pointing a gun. Old cases indicate that there must be an act of some kind and words alone are not enough, but the logic of this is questioned now.

The question of what comes within the *actus reus* is not an easy one.
Authority: *Arobieke* (1987). D had been following his victim and was looking at a train which he thought his victim might have boarded. His victim was not on the train but panicked when he saw D and tried to escape across a railway line. The line was live and the victim was electro-

cuted. The court held the D was not guilty of unlawful act manslaughter because his actions did not constitute an assault. There was no apprehension by the victim of the immediate infliction of violence.

Mens rea of assault

Assault is a crime of basic intent and either recklessness or intention will suffice for *mens rea*.

Recklessness for these purposes is *Cunningham* recklessness (see Chap. 2).

The previous case of *D.P.P.* v. *K* (1989) was overruled by the Court of Appeal, and the House of Lords in *Savage, Parmenter* (1991) has made it clear that the test to be applied is subjective.

Actus reus of battery

The *actus reus* of battery consists of an intentional and hostile touching of, or contact with, one person by another. As in civil law the merest touching of another without his consent is a battery, and may be direct or indirect.

The *actus reus* can be a continuing act.

Authority: *Fagan* v. *Metropolitan Police Commissioner* (1969). D had driven his car on to a policeman's foot by mistake but was slow to remove it when he realised what he had done. The court held that the *actus reus* of the battery was the remaining on the foot and the intention then formed to remain was sufficient *mens rea*.

Mens rea of battery

Battery is a crime of basic intent requiring either intention or recklessness as in assault.

DEFENCES TO ASSAULT AND BATTERY

Reasonable chastisement

Reasonable chastisement by a parent or teacher is a defence although the European Court of Human Rights has ruled that corporal punishment used in schools without parental permission contravenes the Convention.

Consent

Genuine consent may negate liability for battery and some other crimes by virtue of their definition, for example rape.

Mistaken belief in consent, to exonerate, need only be honest and not necessarily reasonable. This is because lack of consent is an element of the offence and a mistake, however unreasonable, regarding lack of consent still negatives a subjective *mens rea* (see Chap. 6).

In *Brown* (1992) (see below), the Court of Appeal appeared to treat consent as a defence. Proof of a victim's consent may sometimes therefore decriminalise an otherwise lawful act. This is much more likely to happen with assault than with the more serious offences where harm is caused. *Brown* itself concerned offences under sections 47 and 20 of the Offences against the Person Act 1861.

Consent must be genuine and not induced by duress, but if it is induced by deception this is irrelevant provided the victim realised what he or she was consenting to.

Authority: *Clarence* (1888). D had intercourse with the victim with her consent. He knew he was suffering from venereal disease but did not tell her. The court held that there was no assault because she had freely consented and knew what she was consenting to.

> "The only cases where fraud indisputably vitiates consent . . . are cases of fraud as to the nature of the act done."

(*per* Stephen L.J.).

Private defence

The amount of force used must be reasonable and is judged objectively, but the basic right in a given situation to defend oneself is judged subjectively and an honest but unreasonable belief in the right to defend oneself is an answer to a charge of assault or battery. This is strictly speaking not a defence but a lack of *actus reus* or *mens rea* because one of the circumstances, (unlawfulness) is not present or the defendant did not have the necessary *mens rea* in relation to that circumstance (see Chap. 6).

STATUTORY OFFENCES

Offences Against the Person Act 1861, section 47

This makes it an offence punishable with up to five years imprisonment to assault another causing that other actual bodily harm. The assault here, as with indecent assault, almost always consists of a battery.

The *actus reus* is that for common law "assault" (*i.e.* battery) plus the consequence of bodily harm. The *mens rea* is the same as for assault.

No *mens rea* at all is required as to the causing actual bodily harm. All that need be proved is the causal link between the assault and the harm, (see *Savage*, below).

Bodily harm has been given a wide interpretation in some cases.

Authority: *Miller* (1954). Harm was defined to include injury to the victim's state of mind.

In *Dawson* (see below), harm for the purposes of unlawful act manslaughter was defined much more narrowly, and the kind of nervous shock mentioned in *Miller* was excluded.

Offences Against the Person Act 1861, section 20

Under this section:

"Whosoever shall unlawfully and maliciously wound or inflict any grievous bodily harm upon any other person either with or without any weapon or instrument shall be guilty of an offence . . ."

Actus reus. There are two alternative offences here: inflicting grievous bodily harm and wounding. Wounding is a fairly straightforward offence. It involves breaking the skin even if only in a minor form such as a graze. "Inflict" had long been thought to predicate an "assault" (*i.e.* battery). In the *Clarence* situation, for example, because the act which caused the harm was with consent, this did not constitute an assault. However, this is no longer a requirement.

Authority: *Wilson* (1984). The House of Lords held that the word "inflict" included doing something directly resulting in force being violently applied to the victim's body. It was therefore wider than assault. The House of Lords in *Savage* indicated that an alternative verdict under section 47 was nearly always possible.

"Grievous" means serious harm. If only slight harm is caused the defendant should be charged under section 47.

Authority: *D.P.P.* v. *Smith* (1961). D had stopped his car to be questioned by a police constable. He accelerated suddenly and the constable clung to the car. D zigzagged trying to shake him off and eventually he was thrown into the path of a passing car and was killed. The House of Lords in defining grievous bodily harm said that the words must have their ordinary natural meaning. "Bodily harm" need no explanation and "grievous" meant no more nor less than really serious. The trial judge's direction in terms of serious harm was held not to be a misdirection.

This was confirmed in the case of *Saunders* (1985), where the Court of Appeal said that there was no real difference between the meaning of "serious" and "really serious," and a direction in terms of serious injury was sufficient.

Mens rea. An offence under section 20 is one of basic intent. The word "maliciously" means intentionally or recklessly where the defendant foresaw the possible consequences (*i.e. Cunningham* and not *Caldwell* recklessness). Foresight of some harm, however slight, suffices although the harm actually caused must be serious.

Authority: *Savage, Parmenter* (1991). In *Savage*, D had thrown beer at her victim, and as she put down the glass it smashed and some pieces struck the victim, injuring her. It was held that for liability under section 47, it was not necessary that she foresaw the risk of this happening, provided that she had the necessary *mens rea* for the assault, which she did. There is an issue on the facts as to whether the assault was a cause of the eventual injury, but this was not picked up by the courts.

In *Parmenter*, D had caused injury to his young baby by tossing him about in a way which would have been acceptable with an older child, but not with one so young. He did not realise that he might cause harm by this action. The House of Lords held that he could not be liable under section 20 as he had not forseen the risk of any harm. It was not necessary under section 20 that he forsee the grievous bodily harm which must be caused, but D must forsee that he might cause some harm. An alternative verdict under section 47 was substituted.

"Unlawfully" admits possible "defences" of consent or self-defence which would negate the unlawfulness of the act.

Authority: *Brown* (1992). Ds were involved in a series of sado-masochistic sexual acts, carried out consensually in private. They had videoed the acts, and the police seized the video. They were charged with offences under sections 47 and 20 of the 1861 Act. The Court of Appeal, affirming their convictions, held that the fact of consent was sometimes but not always relevant. It was a matter of public policy whether a victim could consent to harmful acts carried out against him, and would depend on the circumstances. Here, despite the private nature of the acts, there was "no good reason" for the infliction of harm, and the harm was more than just transient. For these reasons the consent was irrelevant and the defendants were liable.

Offences Against the Person Act 1861, section 18

This section provides:

> "Whosoever shall unlawfully and maliciously by any means whatsoever wound or cause any grievous bodily harm to any person, with intent to do some grievous bodily harm to any person, or with intent to resist or prevent the lawful apprehension or detainer of any person, shall be guilty of an offence . . ."

Wounding and grievous bodily harm have the same meanings as under section 20.

Under section 18 the defendant must have *caused* grievous bodily harm as opposed to inflicted it. It is unclear what the difference is, if any, between the two now that there is no longer a requirement under section 20 that the harm always be caused by an assault.

Mens rea. A section 18 offence is a specific intent offence. "Maliciously" and "unlawfully" bear the same meaning as in section 20, but ulterior intent must be proved.

There are two forms of this intent:
  (i)   an intent to do some grievous bodily harm, or
  (ii) an intent to resist or prevent a lawful arrest or detention.

Recklessness as to doing grievous bodily harm with intent is insufficient for liability.

Authority: *Belfon* (1976). The Court of Appeal held that merely foreseeing probable grievous bodily harm (*i.e.* *Cunningham* recklessness) is insufficient for liability. The defendant must either intend or foresee the consequence as a moral certainty.

Under section 18, intention to cause serious harm is necessary. Unlike section 20, it is not enough if the defendant intended only slight harm.

SEXUAL OFFENCES AGAINST THE PERSON

Sexual offences as a separate topic is not often included in an undergraduate syllabus but because of recent developments in the law of rape, particularly with regard to *actus reus* and *mens rea* and mistake, a knowledge of the law relating to rape is particularly important.

Rape

Section 1(1) of the Sexual Offences Act 1956 provides that it is an offence for a man to rape a woman.

Section 1(1) of the Sexual Offences (Amendment) Act 1976 provides that

> ". . .a man commits rape if—
> (a)   he has unlawful sexual intercourse with a woman who at the time of the intercourse does not consent to it; and
> (b)   at that time he knows that she does not consent to the intercourse or he is reckless as to whether she consents to it . . ."

This in effect affirms the common law and *Morgan* v. *D.P.P.* (see below).

Actus reus. The *actus reus* of rape is sexual intercourse without the woman's consent.

Until recently there was an additional requirement that the intercourse be unlawful, meaning outside marriage, but that is no longer the case.

Authority: *R* (1992). D had intercourse with his wife without her consent. They had been living apart, but he forced his way into the house where she was living, and forced her to have intercourse with him. He was found guilty and appealed. Both the Court of Appeal and the House of Lords affirmed the conviction. It was held that the word "unlawful" no longer had any meaning in the context of this offence. Although the common law rule had been for many years that a man could not be liable for raping his wife, the common law changed and developed with changing social attitudes and morals, and given that modern marriage was a partnership of equals, the common law rule had changed to match this. Although the word "unlawful" had been included in the 1976 Sexual Offences (Amendment) Act, their Lordships held that this was merely the draughtsman's way of allowing for continuing develoment of the common law, and therefore did not have any significance. The effect of the case therefore is to bring about in practice a major change in the law of rape. It was irrelevant, according to the judgements, whether husband and wife

were living together or apart; all non-consensual intercourse was rape.
By section 44 of the 1956 Act:

> ". . . it shall not be necessary to prove the completion of intercourse by the emission of seed, but the intercourse shall be deemed complete upon proof of penetration only."

The slightest penetration suffices and intercourse is a continuing act. Where during intercourse a man realises the woman is not, or is no longer, consenting, then the defendant now has the necessary *mens rea* for the offence and the continuing of intercourse is the *actus reus*.

Authority: *Kaitamaki* (1985). (See Chap. 2.)

Lack of consent is an element of the offence which must be proved by the prosecution. "Consent" must not be obtained by intimidation.

Authority: *Olugboja* (1952). D's victim submitted to sexual intercourse with him through fear of what might happen if she did not. The court held that the consent was not genuine.

Deception is rather more difficult. Inducing a married woman to have intercourse by impersonating her husband is deemed rape by section 1(2) of the 1956 Act. Otherwise, only deceiving the woman as to the *nature* of sexual intercourse suffices to negate consent, and other types of deception as in *Clarence* (see above) do not, even if, had the facts been known, the woman would not have consented. However, procuring women to have intercourse by threats, false pretences or by administering drugs, etc. are separate offences under sections 24 of the 1956 Act.

Mens rea. Rape is a crime of basic intent. A man will be guilty if either he knows the woman does not consent or he is reckless as to whether she consents. It is clear from the decision of the House of Lords in *Morgan* that the test should be subjective.

Authority: *D.P.P.* v. *Morgan and others* (1976) (see Chap. 6 for facts). The House of Lords held that if the defendants honestly believed the woman consented they would not be liable, however unreasonable that belief was. They were not reckless as to whether or not she consented if they honestly believed that she did consent.

Immediately after the decision in *Caldwell* (see Chap. 2), there were suggestions in some cases that objective recklessness might be sufficient, but the subjective test was finally confirmed by the Court of Appeal.

Authority: *Satnam* (1984). (See Chap. 2, above.)

Reforms

In March 1992 the Law Commission issued a Consultation Paper (No. 122) in which the following major recommendations were made concerning non-fatal violence offences.

  1.   Clause 8 sets out the offence of assault which would replace the separate offences of assault and battery, and encompass them

both. The act must be non-consensual unless it is intended or likely to cause injury, where consent would be irrelevant. The clause specifically excludes kinds of contact deemed normally acceptable as part of life within a community.

2. Clause 4 sets out the most serious offence which would be the intentional causing of serious injury.

3. Clause 5 would create an offence of recklessly (meant subjectively) causing serious injury.

4. Clause 6 would create an offence of either intentionally or recklessly causing injurey.

5. Injury is defined in clause 1 to cover both physical and mental injury, including pain and unconsciousness.

Immediately following the decision in *R.*, the Law Commission issued its Report on Rape within Marriage (No. 205), suggesting that the reform carried out by the case be codified, and other procedural reforms enacted at the same time.

SUMMARY

The main topics for revision are:

Assault and battery
Actus Reus of Assault (*Arobieke*)
Mens Rea of Assault (*Savage, Parmenter*)
Actus Reus of Battery (*Fagan* v. *M.P.C.*)
Mens Rea of Battery

Defences to assault and battery
Reasonable Chastisement
Consent (*Brown, Clarence*)
Private Defence

Statutory offences
Section 47, Offences Against the Person Act 1861 (*Miller*)
Section 20, Offences Against the Person Act
Actus Reus (*Wilson, Savage, Parmenter, D.P.P.* v. *Smith*)
Mens Rea (*Savage, Parmenter*)
Section 18, Offences Against the Person Act
Mens Rea (*Belfon*)

Sexual offences against the person
Rape
Section 1, Sexual Offences Act 1956
Section 1, Sexual Offences (Amendment) Act 1976

Actus Reus (*R.*, section 44, S.O.A. 1956, *Kaitamaki*, *Olugboja*)
Mens Rea (*Morgan*, section 1, S.O.A.A. 1976)
Caldwell or *Cunningham* Recklessness (*Satnam*)

Reforms
Law Commission Consultation Paper on Non-fatal Offences (No. 122, 1992)
Law Commission Report on Rape within Marriage (No. 205, 1992)

---

8. HOMICIDE

Homicides are unlawful killings. The major categories are murder, manslaughter and causing death by dangerous driving.

MURDER

Murder, basically a common law offence, is the unlawful killing of a human being under the Queen's peace with malice aforethought so that the victim dies within a year and a day.

Actus reus
The killing must be of a human being. The unlawful killing of an unborn child therefore is not murder and is covered by other offences.

"Under the Queen's peace" means that the killing of an enemy in the course of war will not be murder.

The killing must be unlawful. Certain defences (see Chap. 6), for example self-defence, will make a killing lawful.

The death must occur within a year and a day of the defendant's conduct. This is an historical left-over from the days when causation was often more difficult to prove but it is still a requirement for the offence (see *Dyson*, and generally Chap. 1).

Mens rea
Mens rea generally is dealt with in Chap. 2, and many of the points made there are particularly relevant to murder. The *mens rea* for murder is defined as malice aforethought but it has been unclear in the past exactly what this means. Its meaning has been made clearer by recent House of Lords decisions.

Authority: *Moloney* (1985). Moloney, a soldier, had become involved in a heated discussion with his step-father about guns. His step-father had teased him that he would not dare to fire a live bullet at which point Moloney fired a loaded shotgun at him and killed him.

The case turned on the definition of malice aforethought and the interpretation of *Hyam*. The House of Lords held that nothing less than intention to kill or cause grievous bodily harm would constitute malice aforethought: merely foreseeing the victim's death as probable was insufficient, and on that basis the conviction for murder was quashed and a manslaughter conviction was substituted.

Hyam, the previous leading authority, had defined intention or malice aforethought (it was unclear which) in terms of foresight of probable consequences, and therefore although *Moloney* does not expressly overrule *Hyam*, this is its effect.

Intention. Murder is an offence of specific intent. It is now clear that recklessness is insufficient *mens rea*, whereas from the speeches in *Hyam* it was unclear whether foreseeing death or grievous bodily harm as likely constituted reckless murder.

Intention in this context includes direct or oblique intent. Direct intent covers the situation where the defendant desired the consequence. In that case the *likelihood* of death or grievous bodily harm occurring is irrelevant.

Oblique intent covers the situation where the consequence is foreseen by the defendant as virtually certain, although not desired for its own sake.

Foresight of consequences. This concept has caused considerable problems in the law relating to murder. At one stage it seemed that a person was deemed to have intended the natural and probable consequences of his acts, but this is no longer the case.

Section 8 of the Criminal Justice Act 1967 provides that a person is not to be taken as intending the natural and probable consequences of his act simply because they were natural and probable, although a jury *may* infer that from looking at all the evidence. The test therefore is subjective and a jury is to decide what the defendant's intention was from considering all the evidence.

The situation had been reasonably clear, but Lord Bridge's speech in *Moloney* where he talked about foresight of natural consequences indicating intention, although not a reversion to the *D.P.P.* v. *Smith* rule, was couched in sufficiently wide terms to possibly mislead a jury.

Authority: *Hancock* (1986). Ds dropped a concrete block over a motorway bridge. It struck a taxi passing underneath and the driver was killed. The taxi was carrying strike-breaking miners to work and the defendants were striking miners who wanted to prevent the other miners getting to the pit. The trial judge directed the jury on the basis of Lord Bridge's statements in *Moloney* and the defendants were convicted of murder.

On appeal a verdict of manslaughter was substituted by the House of Lords. Lord Scarman stated that a jury should be directed in more detailed terms than Lord Bridge's statement in *Moloney*, and the effect of section 8 of the Criminal Justice Act reiterated. The more likely a consequence, the more likely it is foreseen; the more likely it is foreseen, the more likely it is intended, *but that is all*. It is a question for the jury to decide as a matter of fact on all the evidence and not a matter of law.

This has also been confirmed by the Court of Appeal in *Nedrick* (see Chap. 2).

Intention to cause grievous bodily harm. This category of malice aforethought for murder is unusual in that it allows a conviction for murder, the most serious of crimes, when the defendant did not intend to kill or even forsee that death was a possible result of his acts.

Although the rule was questioned by several judges, notably in *Hyam*, the House of Lords in *Moloney* expressly confirmed it and it is now well established, although narrower than was previously thought, given the restricted definition of intention in that case.

Reform

The Law Commission in the Draft Criminal Code re-defines murder. A person will be guilty of murder if he intends to cause death, or if he intends to cause serious injury and is aware that death may result. It would no longer therefore be murder where a defendant intends to cause serious injury but does not realise subjectively the risk of death.

VOLUNTARY MANSLAUGHTER

There are two kinds of manslaughter: voluntary and involuntary manslaughter.

Voluntary manslaughter covers the situations where the defendant has the necessary *mens rea* and *actus reus* for murder but certain kinds of extenuating circumstances partially excuse his conduct.

The two main kinds of voluntary manslaughter are murder reduced to manslaughter on the ground of provocation, and murder reduced to manslaughter on the ground of diminished responsibility. They are both governed by the Homicide Act 1957. They are not charged as offences in themselves but act as partial defences to murder charges.

Although these extenuating circumstances may exist in the commission of any crime, the Homicide Act only applies to murder. This is because there is a fixed penalty for murder and there is therefore no judicial sentencing discretion. In any other crime the judge can take extenuating circumstances into account and reduce sentence accordingly.

Provocation

Under section 3 of the Homicide Act 1957:

"Where on a charge of murder there is evidence on which the jury can find that the person charged was provoked (whether by things done or by things said or by both together) to lose his self-control, the question whether the provocation was enough to make a reasonable man do as he did shall be left to be determined by the jury; and in determining that question the jury shall take into account everything both done and said according to the effect which, in their opinion, it would have on a reasonable man."

Provocation as a means of reducing murder to manslaughter existed before the Homicide Act but the rules were much more restrictive in terms of the time-scale of reaction, the kind of provocation and the proportionality of the reaction.

The Act makes it clear that the jury must decide the case on matters of fact and the above-mentioned matters would merely be of evidential value for the jury in deciding whether the defendant was provoked and whether a reasonable man in his position would have reacted as he did.

The defendant does not have to *prove* provocation: if the jury has a reasonable doubt as to whether he was provoked, he is entitled to the benefit of the doubt.

Loss of self-control is often an immediate response to the provocation, but that is not required as a matter of law. It is a question of fact whether it was the provocation which caused the loss of self-control, and the closer they are in time, the easier it is to prove.

Authority: *Ahluwaliah* (1992). D had set fire to her husband while he was sleeping. She had been a victim of domestic violence for many years, but her response to her husband's violence was not immediately following any specific act. The Court of Appeal held (*inter alia*) that there must be a sudden and temporary loss of self-control, but it need not immediately follow the provocative act or acts. Nevertheless it was held that there was no misdirection on this point by the trial judge.

Was the defendant provoked? This matter is judged subjectively. The judge will decide whether there is sufficient evidence on which a jury could find provocation, and if there is he must leave the matter to them. He must put the issue to the jury even if the defendant does not raise it himself. It is then up to the jury to decide whether the defendant was in fact provoked. If he was not, it is irrelevant that a reasonable man would have been.

Authority: *Rossiter* (1992). D was a victim of domestic violence over a period of years. In response to an attack by her husband which was not life-threatening she lost control and stabbed him many times, killing him. Her defence of self-defence was rejected by the jury, but on appeal the Court of Appeal held that according to section 3 of the Homicide Act it was the duty of the judge to put the issue of provocation to the jury, even if not raised by the defence. There was evidence on which a jury might find she lost her self-control, and therefore a verdict of manslaughter was substituted.

The "reasonable man" test. The second element of the provocation test is objective. Having decided that the defendant was provoked, the jury must decide whether a reasonable man would have acted as the defendant did.

The reasonable man test was until fairly recently interpreted strictly. The reasonable man was attributed with none of the defendant's particular characteristics which might be relevant to the provocation. The test was reinterpreted by the House of Lords.

Authority: *D.P.P.* v. *Camplin* (1978). D, aged 15, had been drinking. He said he had been homosexually assaulted and was then laughed at and taunted by his victim. D lost control, hit his victim over the head with a pan and killed him. The House of Lords held that certain characteristics of the accused, such as his intoxication or excitability, would be ignored for policy reasons, but other characteristics which were relevant to the provocation should be attributed to the reasonable man when a jury asked whether a reasonable man would have reacted as the defendant did.

In this case the reasonable man would be the reasonable 15 years old, as D's youth was a relevant characteristic. His drunkenness was irrelevant, however.

The Court of Appeal has indicated that the reasonable person means the reasonable person who is suffering from "battered woman syndrome" in an appropriate case, provided there is sufficient medical evidence.

Authority: *Ahluwalia* (1992) (see above). The Court of Appeal in this case referred to cases heard in the New Zealand courts where this had been raised, and likened it to post-traumatic stress disorder cases, where medical evidence has recently been admitted to establish a medical condition not previously recognised.

Self-induced provocation. If the defendant induces the provocation by some act of his own then it is much more difficult to rely on provocation as a defence, and the provocation must be extreme compared with the original act for the defence to apply, but provocation is not automatically unavailable as a defence simply because it is self-induced.

Authority: *Johnson* (1989). The victim and the appellant had been drinking. The appellant used threatening behaviour towards his victim, and the victim used insulting words and behaviour towards the appellant. A struggle developed resulting in the death of the victim. The appellant pleaded reasonable self defence, because he thought he would be hit by a glass. The appellant was convicted of murder, and appealed on the grounds that the judge should have left the issue of provocation to the jury. The Court of Appeal substituted a manslaughter verdict, saying that the fact that the defendant induced the provocation himself, which caused him to lose self-control, did not mean that provocation should not be put as a defence to the jury. Self-induced provocation could be relevant in some circumstances, and it was conceivable that the jury might have believed the provocation defence if it had been left to them.

Diminished responsibility

If a defendant can prove on a balance of probabilities a defence of diminished responsibility, he will be guilty of manslaughter rather than murder under section 2(1) of the Homicide Act 1957 which states:

> "Where a person kills or is party to the killing of another, he shall not be convicted of murder if he was suffering from such abnormality of mind (whether arising from a condition of arrested or retarded development of mind or any inherent causes or induced by disease or injury) as substantially impaired his mental responsibility for his acts and omissions in doing or being a party to the killing."

This was a completely new concept introduced by the Homicide Act because of the unsatisfactory definition of insanity under the M'naghten Rules (see Chap. 6).

Abnormality of mind. An abnormality of mind is a state of mind which the reasonable man would consider abnormal. It is therefore defined very widely and covers many conditions which are not covered by the insanity defence.

Authority: *Byrne* (1960). D had strangled his victim and then mutilated her body. He claimed he was subject to an irresistible or almost irresistible impulse because of perverted sexual desires which overcame him and had done so since he was a boy.

The Court of Appeal quashed his conviction for murder because the trial judge had misdirected the jury that section 2 of the 1957 Act was irrelevant here. The Court said that the defence covered the mind's activities in all its aspects and the ability to control one's physical acts. This would cover the irresistible impulse situation.

Abnormality of mind has been held to cover severe shock or depression common in mercy-killing cases and "battered wife syndrome." (See *Ahluwalia*, above.) Section 2, like section 3, gives a large amount of discretion to the jury. It is unnecessary that the abnormality be "borderline madness."

Authority: *Seers* (1984). D had stabbed his estranged wife. He raised the defence of diminished responsibility because of his chronic reactive depression. His conviction for murder was quashed, the judge having misdirected the jury in terms of diminished responsibility as partial insanity or bordering on the insane.

How the abnormality arises. This too is very widely defined. It covers:

(i) A condition of arrested or retarded development of mind.
(ii) Any inherent causes.

(iii)   Disease or injury.

Although this excludes drink or drugs it does cover disease caused by long term alcoholism or drug-taking.

Authority: *Gittens* (1984). D suffered from depression and had been in hospital. On a visit home he had an argument with his wife and he clubbed her to death. He then raped and killed his step-daughter. He had been drinking and taking drugs for medication. The jury had to try and discount the effect of alcohol and decide whether the inherent causes themselves would have caused the defendant to act as he did.

The abnormality of the mind must be induced by one of the causes mentioned above.

Authority: *Tandy* (1987). The defendant was an alcoholic. On this particular day she drunk much more than normal, and she strangled her daughter. She did not claim that she could not stop herself from drinking, and admitted that she was able to exercise some control over her drinking initially. The judge withdrew the diminished responsibility defence from the jury. She appealed, but the appeal was dismissed. The Court held that the abnormality of the mind which resulted in the killing had to be induced by the alcoholism in order for the defence to apply. In order for the craving for alcohol to produce the abnormality of mind, it must be such as to render the use of alcohol involuntary, and this was not the case here, as the defendant admitted having some control over whether she had that first drink. The defence should therefore not be left to the jury in such circumstances.

The effect of the abnormality of mind. The abnormality of mind must substantially impair the defendant's mental responsibility. The impairment therefore need not be total. The defendant may know what he is doing, know it is wrong, and have some control over himself but find it substantially *more* difficult than a normal person would to control his actions. This difficulty in controlling oneself must obviously be caused by the abnormality of mind.

Authority: *Byrne* (see above). The evidence in the case was not that D found the impulse irresistible but that he found it very difficult to control. This suffices under the 1957 Act.

Reforms

The Draft Criminal Code recommends minor changes to the existing forms of voluntary manslaughter, and one addition to the category.

In deciding the question of provocation, the defendant is to be judged on the facts as he believed them to be, and regard is to be had to all circumstances and personal characteristics. The test therefore becomes more subjective, in line with self-defence.

When deciding whether diminished resonsibility should apply, there should be such mental abnormality as is a substantial enough reason to reduce murder to manslaughter. Mental abnormality is defined in the Code.

In addition to the existing categories of voluntary manslaughter, the Code would introduce a third category—the use of excessive force in self-defence. Where the defendant believes it necessary and reasonable to defend himself, but the amount of force he uses is excessive in the circumstances that exist or that he believes to exist, then he will be liable for manslaughter rather than murder. (See also Chap. 6.)

A defendant would also be liable under the Draft Code for attempted manslaughter where, had his victim died, he would have been guilty of voluntary manslaughter.

INVOLUNTARY MANSLAUGHTER

Involuntary manslaughter is the term given to an unlawful homicide where the necessary *mens rea* for murder is not present. There are two main kinds of involuntary manslaughter, although recent case law has blurred the distinction: unlawful act manslaughter, and manslaughter by gross negligence or recklessness.

Constructive or unlawful act manslaughter

If D has committed an unlawful act which a reasonable person would realise creates a risk of injury, and death results, then he is guilty of manslaughter. This is a constructive liability as the defendant need not foresee the risk of death, nor need it be reasonably forseeable.

Authority: *Church* (1966). D attacked a woman and knocked her out. Unable to revive her he threw her in a river believing her to be dead. In fact she was alive when he did so, but she subsequently drowned. The Court of Appeal held that it was not necessary that the defendant himself should have realised the risk, only that ordinary sober and reasonable people would have realised the risk of some harm.

Actus reus. The *actus reus* consists of the unlawful act which creates the risk of harm. Although the harm risked need not be serious it must be physical harm of some kind.

Authority: *Dawson* (1985). D and others attempted to rob a filling station attendant but ran away when he raised the alarm. The victim however had heart trouble and the stress of the incident caused him to have a heart attack and die. On appeal against a conviction for manslaughter the Court of Appeal held that harm in this context meant physical and not emotional harm, although shock or stress which resulted in physical harm sufficed. The Court also held that the reasonable man must be taken to know only the facts and circumstances which the defendant knew. He would not know in this case that the victim had a weak heart because the defendant did not know that. The conviction for manslaughter was quashed because of the judge's misdirections.

The unlawful act itself, although originally very widely defined to cover torts as well as crimes, now seems limited to criminal offences. It does not cover acts or omissions which are unlawful only because they are negligent.

Authority: *Andrews* v. *D.P.P.* (1937). D was charged with manslaughter. He had been driving dangerously and knocked over and killed someone. The House of Lords differentiated between manslaughter by unlawful act and manslaughter by gross negligence and said that an act which was criminal only because of the negligent manner in which it was performed was not a sufficiently unlawful act for unlawful act manslaughter.

Neither does an unlawful omission seem at present to be enough for unlawful act manslaughter, although there is no reason in principle why this should be so. It seems rather to be a policy decision.

Authority: *Lowe* (1973). D was guilty of an unlawful omission under the Children and Young Persons Act 1933. He had neglected to care for his child, and that neglect resulted in death. The Court held that such an unlawful omission should not automatically lead to liability for manslaughter, which it would do if it were an act. This is still the authority on manslaughter by unlawful omission.

Mens rea. The *mens rea* for this type of manslaughter consists of negligence as to the risk of harm, and intention or recklessness as to the unlawful act itself, depending on what the necessary *mens rea* is for the act.

The defendant need not therefore subjectively realise the risk of causing some harm; as long as the reasonable man in his position would have so realised this is sufficient *mens rea*.

In cases where only *Caldwell* recklessness, involving an objective test, need be proved for the unlawful act, for example criminal damage, it will be easier to prove unlawful act manslaughter than manslaughter by gross negligence, because in unlawful act manslaughter the harm foreseeable need only be slight, whereas in manslaughter by gross negligence it must be an obvious and serious risk of injury or death.

If the unlawful act is one of the offences against the person, then the subjective test of recklessness will apply.

Manslaughter by gross negligence or recklessness

Manslaughter by gross negligence occurs where an act, otherwise lawful, is carried out, or an omission occurs, in circumstances of negligence which go beyond the ordinary civil law concept of negligence, and the behaviour is so extreme that it warrants criminal liability. Whether the requisite degree of negligence is reached is up to a jury.

If negligence is sufficient for liability it follows that recklessness, while insufficient for liability for murder, will suffice for this category of manslaughter.

Authority: *Kong Chuek Kwan* (1985). The Privy Council said that in gross negligence manslaughter, the questions the jury must answer are:

   (1)   did D's conduct create an obvious and serious risk of causing injury, and, if so,

   (2)   did he give no thought to the possibility of that risk, or while he recognised that risk, did he take it?

This test covers both negligence and *Caldwell* recklessness.

Mens rea. The *mens rea* is objective. The defendant will be liable if the reasonable man could foresee an obvious and serious risk of injury. It is not absolutely clear what "obvious and serious" means, but it probably means a high risk of serious injury. *Kong Cheuk Kwan* is a clarification of Lord Roskill's explanation of this in *Seymour*.

Authority: *Seymour* (1983). D had had a quarrel with his girlfriend and he hit her car with his lorry. She got out to speak to him and as she stood between the car and the lorry he drove into her car again, crushing her between the two vehicles and she died.

Because the fact situation was so serious the prosecution charged manslaughter instead of causing death by reckless driving.

The House of Lords stated that this was a "motor manslaughter" case and it would be nonsensical to have a different definition of recklessness to that used in causing death by reckless driving. The relevant definition, according to *Lawrence*, was *Caldwell* recklessness. The correct *mens rea* requirement here was therefore *Caldwell* recklessness, although in respect of manslaughter the alternative forseeable risk of damage to property is irrelevant. The forseeable risk must be of injury to the person. Lord Roskill's requirement of forseeability of death, mentioned in *Seymour*, is withdrawn in *Kong Cheuk Kwan*.

According to the House of Lords in this case, therefore, the necessary *mens rea* for reckless manslaughter is *Caldwell* recklessness as to some harm, that is to say, there must be an obvious and serious risk of harm, and;

   (i)   either the defendant must have realised that risk and decided to take it,

   (ii)   the defendant gave no thought to what was an obvious and serious risk of some harm.

Given that the House of Lords has now, *obiter dicta*, indicated that the *Caldwell* "loophole" or lacuna has virtually no relevance (*Reid*), the difference between objective recklessness and negligence is now, if it exists at all, only a matter of the seriousness of the risk. Manslaughter by gross negligence and recklessness are thus virtually the same.

Reforms

The Code proposes major reforms to involuntary manslaughter, moving away from negligent, objective based manslaughter altogether. A person will be guilty of involuntary manslaughter if because of voluntary intoxication he is not aware that death may be caused, or he believes an exempting circumstance exists, OR

he causes death intending serious personal harm, OR

he is reckless whether death or serious personal harm is caused.

This therefore provides an entirely subjective basis for involuntary manslaughter. Manslaughter by gross negligence and *Caldwell* recklessness would be abolished, as would unlawful act manslaughter as a separate category.

CAUSING DEATH BY DANGEROUS DRIVING

Under section 1 of the Road Traffic Act 1991:

> "A person who causes the death of another person by driving a mechanically propelled vehicle dangerously on a road or other public place is guilty of an offence."

The concept of dangerousness replaces that of recklessness. It relates both to the manner of driving and to the defendant's state of mind. A person drives dangerously if the way he drives (or the state of his vehicle) falls far below what would be expected of a competent and careful driver, and it would be obvious to a competent and careful driver that driving in that way would be dangerous. The danger involved would be danger of injury or serious damage to property.

The only subjective element of the test increases rather than decreases the ambit of potential liability, because regard must be had not just to circumstances which would be known to the careful and competent driver, but to any additional circumstances known to the defendant.

Mens rea

Authority: *Lawrence* (see above). The House of Lords also defined the *mens rea* for section 1 of the previous statute in this case, following the definition of recklessness given in *Caldwell*. A driver is reckless if he does not give any thought to the obvious and serious risk or he recognises the risk and decides to take it.

The test for dangerous driving is similarly objectively based, applying a standard of negligence and is wider than the old concept of reckless driving.

In any fact situation where there is an obvious and serious risk of injury, the *actus reus* of this offence and manslaughter coincide, and Lord Roskill's judgement in *Kong Cheuk Kwan* emphasises that his words in *Seymour* are meant as guidance to prosecuting authorities in such cases to help them decide which charge to bring.

SUMMARY

The main topics for revision are:

Murder
  Actus Reus
  Mens Rea (*Moloney*)
  Intention
  Foresight of Consequences (*Hancock*)
  Intention to Cause Grievous Bodily Harm (*Hyam*, *Moloney*)
  Reforms (Draft Criminal Code)

Voluntary manslaughter
  Provocation (section 3, Homicide Act 1957, *Ahluwalia*)
  Was D provoked? (*Rossiter*)
  The Reasonable Man Test (*Camlin*, *Ahluwalia*)
  Self-induced Provocation (*Johnson*)
  Diminished Responsibility (section 2, Homicide Act 1957)
  Abnormality of Mind (*Byrne*, *Seers*)
  How the Abnormality Arises (*Gittens*, *Tandy*)
  Effect of the Abnormality (*Byrne*)
  Reforms (Draft Criminal Code)

Involuntary manslaughter
  Constructive or Unlawful Act Manslaughter(*Church*)
  Actus Reus (*Dawson*, *Andrews*, *Lowe*)
  Mens Rea
  Manslaughter by Gross Negligence (*Kong Chuek Kwan*)
  Mens Rea (*Seymour*, *Reid*)
  Reforms (Draft Criminal Code)

Causing death by dangerous driving
  (section 1, Road Traffic Act 1991)

---

9. THEFT AND RELATED OFFENCES

Theft and the main offences related to it are set out in the Theft Acts 1968 and 1978. This chapter will cover the following: theft, handling, burglary, robbery, blackmail and criminal damage.

THEFT

Under section 1(1) of the 1968 Act:

> "A person is guilty of theft if he dishonestly appropriates property belonging to another with the intention of permanently depriving the other of it."

The offence committed is under section 1. Sections 2–6 provide explanations and definitions of elements of section 1 theft, but do not form separate offences.

Actus reus

The *actus reus* of theft consists of the act of appropriation and the circumstance that the property belonged to another.

Appropriation. Under section 3(1) of the 1968 Act:

> "Any assumption by a person of the rights of an owner amounts to an appropriation . . ."

Although the commonest form of assumption may be taking property away, destroying property, treating property as one's own and selling it are also covered.

The House of Lords has recently been asked to solve the dilemma which has caused difficulty in many cases since two House of Lords decisions, *Lawrence* in 1971 and *Morris* in 1984 appeared to give conflicting interpretations of appropriation. The question at issue is whether an act which is done with the consent of the owner can amount to an appropriation for the purposes of theft, or whether it can only come within the section 15 offence under the 1968 Theft Act of obtaining by deception. The typical situation is where D, using a worthless cheque or draft has bought goods from his victim. Is this theft? The House of Lords has now said that the decision in *Lawrence* is the correct one. Although the decision itself in *Morris* was correct, some parts of the speeches were unnecessary and incorrect. An act can therefore be an appropriation notwithstanding that it was done with the consent of the owner. It was not necessary that there be an adverse interference with or usurpation of some right of the owner. The question was not whether obtaining of property was with the consent of the owner, but whether it was dishonest.

Authority: *Gomez* (1992). D had persuaded his employer to accept what he knew to be a worthless building society cheque in payment for some electrical goods. He was convicted of theft, and appealed on the grounds that because the taking of the goods was with the consent of the owner, there could be no appropriation. Their Lordships held reversing the decision of the Court of Appeal, that the defendant was guilty of theft, because he had obtained the property dishonestly by a false representation, and that was sufficient for appropriation.

Conduct. Conduct of some kind is necessary. An intention on its own is not enough. Under section 3(1) a later assumption of a right, *e.g.* by keeping property after it should be returned, can amount to theft.

Rights of an owner. It is unnecessary that all the rights of an owner be assumed. It is enough that one or some of them are.

Authority: *Morris* (1984), *Anderton* v. *Burnside* (1984). The two Ds' behaviour was similar. In *Morris* D took items from supermarket shelves and replaced the correct labels with ones showing lower prices. He took the items to the checkout and paid the lower price.

In *Anderton* v. *Burnside* D took the label off a joint of meat and placed it on a more expensive joint. His act was discovered before he got to the checkout.

The House of Lords held that as the offence is committed at the moment of appropriation it was irrelevant that D in *Anderton* v. *Burnside* had not left the shop.

Appropriation cannot take place after the defendant has made a contract because ownership of the goods will have passed and the property will no longer belong to another.

Property. Property is defined by section 4 to include real and personal property, money and intangible property, such as credit in a bank account. There are some exceptions under section 4.

Land can only be stolen by a limited group of people in a fiduciary position or by certain persons such as tenants taking something forming part of the land. Wild plants, flowers and mushrooms can only be stolen for commercial purposes, and wild animals cannot be stolen unless they are ordinarily kept in captivity.

Information does not come within the definition of property, and information dishonestly obtained from a computer presented difficulties. This is now covered by the Computer Misuse Act 1990 (see below).

Belonging to another. Under section 5(1), property is regarded as belonging to anyone having possession or control of it or having a proprietary right or interest in it, certain kinds of equitable interest being excluded. The device of a constructive trust cannot be used to catch certain kinds of dishonest behaviour which would not otherwise come within section 1.

Authority: *Attorney General's Reference No. 1 of 1985* (1986). D, a barman sold his own beer to customers. It was argued that the owners of the pub had a proprietary interest in the proceeds of the sale under a constructive trust. The Court rejected this argument saying that this kind of situation was not meant to be covered by section 5(1) and a constructive trust did not arise in this situation.

Property can be stolen from someone in possession or control as well as the person who owns it.

The potential meaning of section 5(1) is very wide.

Authority: *Shadrokh-Cigari* (1988). The appellant was guardian of a minor. Funds for the minor were transferred from an American to an English bank, but the American bank over-credited the account. The appellant got the minor to sign drafts credited to him, and he had spent most of the excess money before he was discovered. He was convicted of theft, and appealed. His appeal was dismissed. The Court held that there were two routes to a conviction. Under section 5(4) (below) he had obtained property by another's mistake, and was therefore liable, but the Court also held that because of the mistake the bank retained an equitable interest in the drafts and therefore the situation was still covered by section 5(1). Section 5(4) was not really necessary.

Provided he has the necessary *mens rea*, a person can steal his own property from someone with a lesser interest.

Authority: *Turner* (1971). D had taken his car to a garage to be repaired. When it was repaired he took it from where it was parked, intending not to pay for the repair. The Court held that the car "belonged to" the repairer at the time D took it as the repairer had control over it. D was therefore guilty of theft.

Receiving property for or on behalf of another. There are some circumstances where legal ownership has passed to the defendant but for the purposes of the Theft Act the property is treated as still belonging to the original owner. Section 5(3) states:

> "Where a person receives property from or on account of another, and is under an obligation to the other to retain and deal with that property or its proceeds in a particular way, the property or proceeds shall be regarded (as against him) as belonging to the other."

This subsection is only relevant where ownership of the goods has passed, and is therefore mainly concerned with money given to a person to deal with in a particular way.

Authority: *Davidge* v. *Bunnett* (1984). D had been given cheques by her flatmates made out to her employer on the understanding that a bill would be paid with the proceeds. D spent the proceeds on christmas presents. The Divisional Court held that D was under a legal obligation to use the proceeds of the cheques in a particular way and therefore they were property belonging to another by virtue of section 5(3). The courts will generally only apply the subsection in the most obvious and straight-forward cases.

Authority: *Hall* (1973). D was a travel agent who had taken money for holidays and not booked them. His business collapsed and the money was lost. Although D had a general obligation to fulfil his contract he did not have to deal with those specific notes and cheques in a particular way and the subsection did not therefore apply.

Authority: *Attorney General's Reference No. 1 of 1985* (1986) (see above). An alternative argument based on section 5(3) was put forward in this case and was also rejected. The Court held that purchasers would hand over their money as part of a contractual obligation and not specifically for the purpose of that money or its proceeds being passed on to the owner.

Receiving property by another's mistake. Under section 5(4):

"Where a person gets property by another's mistake, and is under an obligation to make restoration (in whole or in part) of the property or its proceeds or of the value thereof, then to the extent of that obligation the property or proceeds shall be regarded (as against him) as belonging to the person entitled to restoration. . . ."

This subsection is only applicable when property has passed to the defendant despite the mistake. A mistake as to the identity of the recipient or as to the subject-matter of a contract will make the contract void and ownership will not pass.

Authority: *Attorney General's Reference No. 1 of 1983.* D was mistakenly paid £74 overtime wages by direct debit for work she did not do. When she found out she did nothing. She was charged with theft on the basis of having come by the property by another's mistake. She was acquitted.

The Court held that D had got property (the excess payment) by another's mistake and was under an obligation to deal with it, or the debt, (a chose in action), in a particular way. Section 5(4) therefore applied but appropriation and dishonesty both had to be proved in addition.

The obligation to repay must be a legal one and not merely a moral one.

Authority: *Gilks* (1972). D was paid some excess winnings by a betting shop because of a mistake as to the horse he backed. D realised the mistake but did nothing. The Court of Appeal held that the obligation to repay in this case was not a legal one as contracts with bookmakers are void under the Gaming Act 1845. D's obligation therefore was only a moral one and the subsection did not apply.

Section 5(4) therefore only applies in a small number of situations where:

    (i)   ownership has passed despite a mistake but

   (ii)   there is a legal obligation to rectify the mistake.

If the mistake is induced by fraud or deception then one of the deception offences is likely to be more relevant than theft.

Mens rea of theft

There are two elements of *mens rea* in theft: dishonesty and intention to permanently deprive. Theft is a crime of specific intent, and therefore recklessness as to permanent deprivation will not suffice.

Dishonesty. Dishonesty is partially defined in section 2(1) of the 1968 Act, which sets out the situations where as a matter of law a person is *not* dishonest.

Those situations are:

(i)   Where he believes he has in law the right to deprive the other of the property permanently.

(ii) Where he believes that the other person would have consented to the appropriation if he had known the relevant circumstances: for example unauthorisedly "borrowing" consumable goods from a neighbour or money from a friend's purse.

(iii) (Unless he is a trustee or personal representative), where he acts in the belief that the true owner cannot be found by taking reasonable steps.

Section 2(2) states that a person can be found to be dishonest notwithstanding his willingness to pay for the property. If an owner does not want to sell then it can be dishonest to take the property and leave payment against his will.

Dishonesty not covered by section 2. In situations not covered by section 2, the meaning of dishonesty, as an ordinary word in the English language, is for the jury to decide.

Authority: *Feely* (1973). D took £30 from a shop till. He said he had intended to repay it. The judge directed the jury that D was dishonest in these circumstances but the Court of Appeal held that dishonesty was a question of fact for the jury to decide on the standards of the ordinary decent person.

In more recent cases, more guidance has been given.

Authority: *Ghosh* (1982). The Court set out a two-stage test for dishonesty:

(i)   the jury must decide if the behaviour was dishonest by the standards of the ordinary decent person. If it was not, he is not guilty.

(ii) If the defendant was dishonest by those ordinary decent standards he is only guilty if he *realised* that people would so regard his behaviour.

The test is therefore subjective but does not allow the defendant to claim he is honest when he knows that by the ordinary standards of society people would regard him as dishonest.

Intention permanently to deprive. In some rare situations this intention, although not actually present, will be assumed.

Under section 6(1) of the 1968 Act, such an intention is assumed if a person intends to treat property as his own to dispose of regardless of the other's rights. If the defendant borrows property in such circumstances that it amounts to an outright taking then he is also deemed to treat it as his own.

This covers the situation where the defendant intends to return the property but uses it to such an extent that it is no longer of any use. His borrowing therefore is equivalent to an outright taking as it has the same effect. The commonest example given is that of the season ticket taken, used until it expires, and then returned. It had generally been thought that this subsection would only apply when the thing returned was completely useless or used up. A recent case throws some doubt on this view.

Authority: *Bagshaw* (1988). D had taken some gas cylinders, used up the gas, and then returned the cylinders. He was convicted of theft of the gas cylinders. On appeal the Court of Appeal said that this was a situation where section 6(1) could apply, and it should have been left to a jury to decide whether or not he had used up all the virtue of the cylinders or not. It was perfectly possible that a jury would so decide, but because it had not been put to them, the conviction was quashed.

The subsection only applies in a very small number of cases, and does not cover dishonest borrowing. It does however cover the situation where the defendant sells back the property to the person from whom he has taken it.

Section 6(2) covers an even smaller number of situations and is in fact an explanation of a situation covered by section 6(1). It refers to the situation where a person parts with another's property under a condition for its return which he may not be able to fulfil, and is designed to cover the case where the defendant pawns the property. Despite his intention to retrieve and return the property, he is deemed to treat it as his own.

If a person has a conditional intent to permanently deprive which is not fulfilled because, for example, he can find no property worth stealing in a warehouse or in his victim's pocket, he may commit attempted theft.

HANDLING

Section 22 of the 1968 Act provides that a person is guilty of handling stolen goods if, knowing or believing them to be stolen, and acting other than in the course of stealing, he dishonestly does one of the following:

- (i) Receives the goods.
- (ii) Arranges to receive them.
- (iii) Undertakes their detention, removal, disposal or realisation by or for the benefit of another.
- (iv) Arranges to undertake the above.
- (v) Assists in their detention, removal, disposal or realisation, etc.
- (vi) Arranges to assist in the above.

Actus reus of handling

Receiving or arranging to receive. A person receiving stolen goods may be liable even if he never personally sees or physically handles the goods. He does not have to receive them for the benefit of another, although he may do so. To receive goods which have been stolen will also constitute handling.

Undertaking the retention, removal, disposal or realisation by or for the benefit of another. "Undertaking" implies an act by the defendant carrying out any of the above activities, rather than just tacit agreement or approval. The involvement will be more positive, *e.g.* by transporting goods or selling them. Any such acts must be by or for the benefit of another, normally the thief or another handler.

Arranging to do the above. The goods must actually be stolen by the time the arrangements are made for the offence of handling to be committed. The arranging must be by or for the benefit of another party.

Assisting in the retention, removal, disposal or realisation by or for the benefit of another. "Assisting" implies co-operating with others in carrying out any of the above activities. Verbal assistance will suffice.
Authority: *Kanwar* (1982). D tried to persuade the police that property which she knew to be stolen and retained by her husband, was in fact hers, and that her husband was retaining the property at her request. The Court of Appeal held this could constitute assisting in their retention by or for the benefit of another.

Arranging to do the above. (See heading above.)

For the benefit of another. This requirement distinguishes thieves disposing of property they have stolen, from handlers to whom property is passed, or persons who become involved at a later stage. Such thieves are not therefore automatically handlers. The "other person" concerned is normally the thief.
Authority: *Bloxham* (1983). The House of Lords said that there were two main ways of committing an offence under the section apart from receiving itself: undertaking any of the activities *on behalf of* another.

Handling by omission. There is no liability for omitting to act unless a positive duty to act has arisen in the circumstances. This is in line with the general rule concerning criminal liability for omissions.
Authority: *Pitchley* (1973). D was guilty of handling because he failed to withdraw money from his bank account once he found out that it was stolen. Although he had paid it in innocently, once he knew it was stolen he was under a duty to act, and did not.

Otherwise than in the course of stealing. It is not always easy to spot where theft ends and handling begins, especially as appropriation is seen as a continuing act. It will be a question for the jury to decide on the evidence if there is a possibility of either offence. Where it is clear that either theft or handling has been committed, then a decision that D is innocent of theft is part of the proof that he is guilty of handling.

Authority: *Yip Kai-Foon* (1988). D had allegedly taken part with others in a robbery at a jeweller's store and then attempted to sell on the goods to third parties who turned out to be police officers. The Privy Council held that while it was not acceptable simply to convict him of whichever was the more likely—theft or handling, the jury could use their conclusion of his innocence of theft as proof towards his liability for handling. In handling cases where there is no alternative theft charge it does not have to be proved that the defendant was not a party to the theft.

Goods. These include money and all other property except land (section 34).

Stolen goods. "Stolen goods" as defined by section 24(4) includes goods obtained by blackmail or deception. If the goods are not stolen at the time of the handling then the defendant may only be guilty of attempted handling (see Chap. 5).

Authority: *Park* (1987). D arranged to handle cheques which were to be paid into his account, but at the time of the arrangement the money was not yet stolen. He was convicted of handling and appealed. The Court held that he was not liable, because the goods must be stolen at the time the arrangement is made in order for liability to arise. His conviction was quashed.

Under section 24(3), goods cease to be stolen when they have been restored to the person from whom they were stolen, or to other lawful custody, normally the police.

Authority: *Attorney General's Reference No. 1 of 1974.* A constable had immobilised a car until the owner had returned and he could question him, as he suspected the goods in the car were stolen. The Court held that whether goods were returned to lawful custody in a situation like this depended on the intention of the constable, and whether he had decided to take possession of the goods before the owner returned, or whether he was waiting to see what the owner would say before he decided.

Goods also cease to be stolen if the person from whom they are stolen ceases to have a right to restitution. This right will be lost when someone else gains a good title to the goods. The main situations where this happens are covered by sections 21–25 of the Sale of Goods Act 1979 which set out the exceptions to the rule that a person cannot pass good title if he lacks one himself.

Proceeds of stolen goods. References to stolen goods in the Act include any proceeds of stolen goods which have been in the hands of the thief or handler. Once the proceeds are exchanged by an innocent third party for goods which have *not* been in the hands of the thief or handler, then they are no longer given the label of stolen goods and the chain stops.

Mens rea of handling

Dishonesty. This is a question of fact for the jury to decide, and the same guidelines apply as for dishonesty in theft (see *Ghosh*, above). The partial definition of dishonesty under section 2 does not apply.

Knowledge or belief that the goods are stolen. Knowledge and belief are different states of mind. Either will suffice as *mens rea* for handling, but suspicion is not sufficient.

Authority: *Grainge* (1974). The Court of Appeal held that suspicion did not equal belief, and a wife's strong suspicion that the goods her husband brought home were stolen was not enough to make her a handler.

Suspicion, even coupled with a deliberate shutting of eyes to the possibility of the goods being stolen, does not amount to belief.

Authority: *Moyes* (1984). A judge's direction in terms of deliberate shutting of eyes to the possibility of the goods being stolen equalling belief led to a quashing of the conviction in the Court of Appeal. Belief therefore has a fairly narrow meaning.

Authority: *Hall* (1985). D was found in his mother's flat with stolen goods and two other people who pleaded guilty to burglary. D appealed against conviction on the grounds of misdirection on knowledge or belief. The Court held that D would *know* goods were stolen if he was told by someone with first-hand knowledge, *e.g.* the thief. Belief was something short of knowledge, but only a little short. It applied in the situation where there was no other reasonable conclusion that D could draw from the facts.

Proof of knowledge or belief. Under section 27(3), evidence of the defendant's previous involvement in theft or handling is admissible in some circumstances to help prove knowledge or belief. Evidence of his involvement in handling stolen goods within the last 12 months is admissible, as is evidence of a previous conviction for theft or handling within the last five years.

OTHER OFFENCES UNDER THE 1968 ACT

The following offences, covered by the 1968 Act, are dealt with to some extent in most syllabuses. However, they tend to be covered only briefly, as they are here, being relatively straightforward and presenting few problems.

Robbery

Under section 8(1) of the 1968 Act:

"A person is guilty of robbery if he steals, and immediately before or at the time of doing so and in order to do so, he uses force on any person or puts or seeks to put any person in fear of being then and there subject to force."

Force or fear of force. What distinguishes robbery from theft is the use of force, or putting or seeking to put someone in fear of force. The force must be against the person and not against property.

In order to steal. The force or threat must be used in order to steal. Thus the use of gratuitous violence after a theft, for example would not constitute robbery because the force is not used in order to enable the theft to be carried out.

Immediately before or at the time of stealing. Force, or any threat to use force, must be used at the time of stealing or just before it. The problem of when an offence of theft is completed arises again here. The theft continues until the whole process is completed, which can continue after the actual appropriation and include removing the goods from the immediate vicinity. When the theft is completed is a question of fact for the jury to decide given all the circumstances.

Authority: *Hale* (1979). One D carried out the appropriation while the other tied up the victim in another room. The Court held that theft was a continuing offence and could have continued while the goods were being removed from the premises, which is when the force took place. It was up to the jury to decide on the facts.

Burglary

Under section 9(1) of the 1968 Act burglary can be committed in two ways:

(i) By entering any building or part of a building as a trespasser and with intent to commit theft, grievous bodily harm, rape or criminal damage (section 9(1)(*a*));

(ii) Having entered the premises as a trespasser, by stealing or attempting to steal, or inflicting or attempting to inflict grievous bodily harm (section 9(1)(*b*)).

Section 9(1)(*a*) creates a crime of specific intent. Section 9(1)(*b*) is narrower in the ambit of crimes covered but wider in that no intent is required on entry.

Entry. The entry must be "effective."

Authority: *Brown* (1985). D had been seen by a witness partially inside a broken shop window, his feet still on the ground outside, rummaging through the goods. He was convicted of burglary and appealed on the basis that "entry" meant a complete entry. His appeal was dismissed. The Court held that the entry had to be "effective." Whether it is so depends on the circumstances of the case, and it was obviously effective here. The effect of the earlier case of *Collins*, where it was held that entry had to be effective and substantial, was therefore clarified.

Trespass. Entry as a trespasser must be either intentional or reckless. A person may therefore be a trespasser for the purposes of the civil law but lack the necessary *mens rea* for burglary.

A person will be liable if he enters with permission gained by deception, or with an intention which negates the permission given, *e.g.* by intending to exceed that permission and commit one of the offences referred to in section 9.

Authority: *Jones and Smith* (1976). Ds stole property from the house of a relative which they had permission to enter and use, but the Court held that entry with intent to steal exceeded that permission and therefore was trespass.

Aggravated burglary. Under section 10 of the 1968 Act "aggravated burglary" is committed when the burglar has with him at the time a firearm, imitation firearm, offensive weapon or explosive. Imitation fire-arms would include toy guns, and anything made, adapted or intended to be used as a weapon is covered by the definition. It is necessary to prove that the intention is to use the weapon to cause injury during the burglary, although not necessarily for the purpose of effecting the burglary.

Authority: *Stones* (1989). D had with him at the time of the burglary a kitchen knife which he knew could be used as a weapon, and he intended to use it in self-defence if necessary. The Court held that this was sufficient for liability. The maximum sentence of life imprisonment, as compared with 14 years for burglary, reflects the seriousness of the offence.

Blackmail

Under section 21(1):

> "A person is guilty of blackmail if with a view to gain for himself or another or with intent to cause loss to another, he makes any unwarranted demand with menaces, and for this purpose a demand with menaces is unwarranted unless the person making it does so in the belief—
> (a)   that he has reasonable grounds for making the demand; *and*
> (b)   that the use of the menaces is a proper means of reinforcing the demand."

The main elements of blackmail can be summarised as follows.

Demand with menaces. The demand can be for any act or omission, and can be made in any way , *e.g.* orally, in writing, expressly or by implication.

"Menaces" is said to be easily understood by a jury as an ordinary word of the English language. No detailed judicial guidance is needed therefore, although it must obviously be something detrimental or unpleasant which is likely to influence the ordinary man in the street.

Authority: *Clear* (1968). It was held that the menaces must be something which would influence the ordinary person or which D thought would influence the ordinary person.

With a view to gain or intent to cause loss. Gain and loss are defined in terms of money or property only, although gain includes keeping what one has and loss includes not getting what one might otherwise get.

Unwarranted. The test as to whether a demand is unwarranted is a subjective one. The defendant must believe both that he had reasonable grounds for making the demand and that the means he was using to reinforce his demand were proper.

Authority: *Harvey* (1981). "Proper" was defined to exclude anything which a defendant knows to be unlawful. It is not open to him to say that he felt it was proper and reasonable to break the law to achieve his demand, but it should be left to decide whether he knew that the means he chose were unlawful. Similarly, if he knew what he was doing was morally wrong then he would not be able to claim that he thought the means used were proper.

The burden will be on the prosecution to prove that a defendant did not have the beliefs required.

CRIMINAL DAMAGE

Criminal damage offences are covered by a separate Act of Parliament, the Criminal Damage Act 1971. Although fairly straightforward offences, their significance for the law student has been increased because of the *Caldwell* definition of recklessness.

Under section 1(1) of the 1971 Act:

"A person who without lawful excuse destroys or damages any property belonging to another intending to destroy or damage any such property or being reckless as to whether any such property would be destroyed or damaged shall be guilty of an offence."

The main elements of the offence are as follows.

Actus reus. This consists of destroying or damaging property belonging to another.

Property is defined as tangible property, including land, and therefore differs from property under the Theft Act. "Belonging to another" however has substantially the same meaning as in the 1968 Act, although there is no equivalent to section 5 of that Act.

The destruction or damage must be more than merely nominal, although not necessarily irreversible.

It had been held that a computer disc is damaged within the meaning of the Act if files are deleted from or added to it, but this is no longer the case. The Computer Misuse Act 1990 (see below), requires physical damage in order for liability to arise under the 1971 Act.

Mens rea. The necessary *mens rea* for criminal damage is intention or *Caldwell* recklessness, and is discussed in detail in Chapter 2.

Lawful excuse. Under section 5(2) of the Act a defence of lawful excuse is available if:

(a) the defendant honestly thought he had the consent of the relevant person, or would have if that person had known the circumstances

or

(b) he acted as he did in order to protect property he thought in immediate need of protection, and he believed the means used were reasonable.

The test of such belief is subjective: provided the belief is honest it does not matter that it was unreasonable. See *Jaggard* v. *Dickinson* (Chap. 6).

Destroying or damaging property with intention or recklessness as to endangering life. Under section 1(2) of the Act this is an offence punishable by life imprisonment. The property does not have to belong to another, and the partial definition of lawful excuse in section 5 does not apply, although the general defence of lawful excuse negating *mens rea* does. *Caldwell* recklessness in this context is proved if a reasonable man would have thought there was a risk of endangering life, even if it turns out that no such danger in fact exists.

Authority: *Sangha* (1988). D's actions in setting fire to a flat did not in fact endanger life at all, but the reasonable man would not have realised that at the time, and would have perceived a risk. D did not perceive such a risk, and therefore was liable. The danger to life must come directly from the damage to property and not from some other source.

Authority: *Steer* (1987). D had fired a rifle at a door and window and caused damage to property. He was charged under section 1(2) because of the danger to life from the use of the rifle. On appeal to the House of Lords it was held that the danger to life was from the rifle and not from the damaged property, and this was not sufficient under section 1(2)(*b*) of the Act. The conviction was quashed.

Even if damage to property is slight there can still be liability under this section if there was an obvious risk that the damage would be much greater and thus endanger life.

Authority: *Dudley* (1989). D, following a dispute with neighbours, threw a home-made fire bomb at their door. It erupted in a five foot sheet of flame. The neighbours were able to put out the fire, and only minor damage was caused. The Court held nevertheless that D was liable, as the wording of the statute covered the risk of damage serious enough to endanger life as well as actual damage serious enouh to endanger life.

Arson

Under section 1(3), if either of the above offences under sections (1) and (2) are committed by fire the offence is one of arson punishable by a maximum of life imprisonment.

COMPUTER MISUSE

The law criminalising computer misuse is contained in the Computer Misuse Act 1990.

Under section 1(1) of the Act a person commits an offence if:

(a)   he causes a computer to perform any function with intent to secure access to any program or data held in any computer;

(b)   the access he intends to secure is unauthorised; and

(c)   he knows at the time when he causes the computer to perform the function that this is the case.

This offence is the basic "hacking" offence which does not require actual access or any damage or securing of information. It is a crime of specific intent. D may use one computer to access another, or gain access to one computer in order to access data on that same computer.

Authority: *Attorney General's Ref. No. 1 of 1991 (1992)*. D used a computer in order to gain access to information on it. He was acquitted on the basis that he had not accessed one computer in order to gain access to data on another computer. On a reference by the Attorney General the Court of Appeal ruled that either of the above situations was covered by the statute.

Under section 2 of the Act there is an aggravated offence of committing an offence under section 1 with intent to commit or facilitate the commission of further (arrestable) offences.

Section 3 creates a separate offence of unauthorised modification of the contents of a computer in order to impair operation, reliability or access. This is designed mainly to criminalise the introduction of computer viruses. The possible overlap with criminal damage is removed by section 3(6), which says that no offence is committed under the 1971 Act unless the physical condition of the computer or storage medium is affected.

SUMMARY

The main topics for revision are;

Theft
 Actus Reus
 Appropriation (Gomez) Conduct, rights of an owner (*Morris, Anderton* v. *Burnside*)
 Property Belonging to Another. Section 5(1) (*A.G.'s Ref. No. 1 of 1985, Shadrock-Cigari, Turner*)
 Section 5(3) (*Davidge* v. *Bunnett, Hall, A.G.'s Ref. No. 1 of 1985*)
 Section 5(4) (*A.G.'s Ref. No. 1 of 1983, Gilks*)
 Mens Rea
 Dishonesty (section 2, *Feely, Ghosh*)
 Intention Permanently to Deprive (section 6, *Bagshaw*)

Handling
 Section 22, Theft Act 1968
 Actus Reus
 Receiving or Arranging to Receive
 Undertaking the Retention, etc., of Goods. Arranging to do so
 Assisting in the Retention, etc., of Goods (*Kanwar*). Arranging to do so
 For the Benefit of Another (*Bloxham*)
 Handling by Omission (*Pitchley*)
 Otherwise than in the Course of Stealing (*Yip Kai-Foon*)
 Stolen Goods (*Park, A.G.'s Ref. No. 1 of 1974*)
 Proceeds of Stolen Goods
 Mens Rea
 Dishonesty
 Knowledge or Belief (*Grainge, Moyes, Hall*)
 Proof of Knowledge or Belief

Other offences under the 1968 Act
 Robbery (section 8)
 Force or Fear of Force
 In Order to Steal
 Immediately Before or at the Time of Stealing (*Hale*)
 Burglary (section 9)
 Entry (*Brown*)
 Trespass (*Jones and Smith*)
 Aggravated Burglary (section 10, *Stones*)
 Blackmail (section 21)
 Demand with Menaces (*Clear*)

Gain or Loss
Unwarranted (*Harvey*)

Criminal damage
Criminal Damage Act 1971
Actus Reus, Mens Rea (section 1(1), *Whitely*)
Lawful Excuse (section 5, *Jaggard* v. *Dickinson*)
Intent to Endanger Life (section 1(2), *Sangha, Steer, Dudley*)
Arson (section 1(3))

Computer Misuse
Computer Misuse Act 1990 (*A.G.'s Reference No. 1 of 1991*)

---

10. DECEPTION AND NON-PAYMENT

There are two offences of obtaining by deception under the 1968 Act, and four under the Theft Act 1978.

There is a third offence under the 1978 Act not requiring deception, which is making off without payment.

COMMON ELEMENTS IN DECEPTION OFFENCES

The six deception offences have some elements in common. They all require a deception, a causal link between the obtaining and the deception, and dishonesty. These points are not repeated as each offence is discussed and it is most important to remember that they apply to *all* the deception offences discussed below.

Deception
Deception includes deception by words or conduct, as to fact or law, and includes deception as to the present intentions of any person. Either a deliberate or a reckless deception will suffice.

Authority: *Feeny* (1991). D was a solicitor who had been involved in a mortgage fraud concerning the sale of a house to imaginary persons in order to bump up the price and the mortgage advance. He denied that he had realised what was going on, although he admitted he may have been negligent in his professional judgement. The Court held that D could only be held to be dishonest if he had realised the risk of fraud, and as he was not aware of the risk he could not be counted dishonest. As the deception offences required dishonesty it was therefore apparent that a reckless deception could only occur if D subjectively realised the risk.

Words or conduct

A person's conduct may imply something which turns out to be untrue. This is a sufficient deception.

One of the commonest kinds of conduct deceptions occur where the defendant obtains goods by using a cheque or credit card, knowing that authorisation to use it has been withdrawn. There are particular problems in these cases in proving that the deception caused the obtaining (see below).

Authority: *M.P.C.* v. *Charles* (1976). D used a cheque and cheque card to obtain gaming chips at a gambling club knowing he had exceeded his authorised limit. He was charged with obtaining a pecuniary advantage by deception (section 16(2)(*b*)).

Referring to the deception involved, the House of Lords said that by writing a cheque backed by a cheque card D had impliedly represented that he was authorised to use the card, and his conduct was a sufficient deception.

Authority: *Gilmartin* (1983). D had written some post-dated cheques which were dishonoured as his account was overdrawn on the date. The Court held that the deception here was the implied representation when a cheque is used in payment that it will be honoured in due course.

Deception by omission. There is no general liability for omitting to "undeceive" someone when the defendant has not caused the misapprehension. However, if the defendant by words or conduct has represented something which later becomes untrue, he is under an obligation to correct the misconception.

Authority: *Firth* (1989). D was a doctor who failed to inform the N.H.S. hospital concerned that certain of his patients were private patients. He was therefore not charged for the hospital's services in respect of those patients. The Court held that a deception for these purposes could be by omission to act or speak.

Fact, law or present intentions. A deception can be as to fact, law or present intentions. It may be as to the present intentions of someone other than the defendant.

Cause of obtaining. The deception must be the major cause of the obtaining. If a cheque is backed by a cheque card, is not over the authorised amount, and the seller checks the number and signature, then the cheque will be honoured. It is therefore irrelevant to the seller that he suspects authorisation has been withdrawn.

Authority: *M.P.C.* v. *Charles* (see above). Although it was clear from the evidence that the manager of the gambling club was not influenced by the creditworthiness of D, because he had a cheque card, the House of Lords still held that the deception as to authority to use the card was the operative deception which induced the manager to cash the cheque. This strained interpretation of the facts was necessary in order to avoid an obviously undesirable result.

Authority: *Lambie* (1981). D paid for goods with a Barclaycard knowing her authorisation had been withdrawn. She was charged with obtaining a pecuniary advantage by deception from the bank (under section 16(2)(*a*), now repealed), who were bound to pay the seller. The House of Lords held that the same principle applied to credit cards as to cheque cards, and again in the face of evidence to the contrary they held that the deception as to authorisation had operated on the shop assistant and caused the obtaining of the pecuniary advantage by inducing her to accept the Barclaycard.

It may therefore be that for policy reasons this causal link will be automatically implied in this kind of case.

If the causal link is not present, there may still be liability for an attempt.

Authority: *Laverty* (1970). D sold a car with a false chassis number and number plates. The court held that this deception was not operative on the mind of the buyer when he bought the car, so D was not guilty of obtaining the price of the car by deception. Why a conviction for *attempting* section 15 was not substituted is unclear.

Dishonesty

The guidelines set out in *Ghosh* aply to deception offences too, although section 2 does not.

Authority: *Woolven* (1984). The Court held that where deception was charged there was no need to direct the jury on section 2. A general direction on dishonesty would be wide enough to cover any claim of right D might put forward.

This was confirmed in respect of the offences under the 1978 Act by *Price* (1989).

OBTAINING PROPERTY BY DECEPTION

Under section 15(1) of the 1968 Act:

> "A person who by any deception dishonestly obtains property belonging to another with the intention of permanently depriving the other of it shall . . . be liable . . ."

Actus reus

Property. "Property" covers *all* property and thus has a wider meaning than under section 1, which imposes the limitations regarding land, wild animals and plants.

Obtaining. Obtaining includes getting ownership, possession or control. These are defined in Chapter 9. Property can be obtained for another person, or the deception can allow another person to obtain or retain the property.

Belonging to another. This bears the same meaning as for theft, as set out in section 5(1).

Mens rea

Intention permanently to deprive. This has the same meaning as for theft under section 1. Section 6 is specifically applicable.

Overlap between theft and obtaining property by deception. Where a deception is operative there may also be an appropriation before ownership passes, *e.g.* where the deception is that the property is only borrowed, or in fact situations covered by section 5(3) or (4). However in most deception cases ownership passes before or at an authorised appropriation and therefore the property does not "belong to another" for the purposes of theft.

OBTAINING A PECUNIARY ADVANTAGE BY DECEPTION

Under section 16(1) of the 1968 Act it is an offence to obtain a pecuniary advantage for oneself or another, dishonestly or by deception. The meaning of dishonesty and deception are the same as for section 15. Section 16(2) gives a complete and exclusive definition of pecuniary advantage. The term pecuniary advantage does not have any generalised meaning apart from these specific examples.

Section 16(2)(*b*)

This provision makes it a pecuniary advantage to be allowed to borrow on an overdraft, to take out a policy of insurance or annuity contract, or to obtain better terms for any of these transactions than would otherwise be the case. The word "allowed" is interpreted very widely to cover the situation where the defendant uses a cheque card to create an overdraft without permission, and the bank is obliged to honour the cheque.

Section 16(2)(*c*)

Under this provision it is a pecuniary advantage to be given the opportunity to earn remuneration or greater remuneration in an office or employment, or to win money by betting.

The term employment is interpreted in a general sense.

Authority: *Callender* (1992). D set himself up as a self-employed accountant and deceived clients as to his qualifications. He was charged under section 16(2)(*c*). It was held "employment" covered a contract for services, and therefore covered self-employed people who hired out their services in this way.

OBTAINING SERVICES BY DECEPTION

This is one of three offences created by the Theft Act 1978 to replace section 16(2)(*a*) of the 1968 Act.

Under section 1 it is an offence by deception to dishonestly obtain services from another.

Actus reus

Obtaining of services. This is defined in section 1(2) and occurs where the other person is induced to confer a benefit by doing an act or permitting or causing it to be done on the understanding the benefit will be paid for. If there is no such understanding section 2(1)(*c*) may be appropriate.

If the deception induces the other party to provide a service without any payment then this offence is not committed. There may however be an offence under section 2.

Mens rea
Dishonesty.

EVASION OF LIABILITY BY DECEPTION

Section 2(1) contains three offences although there is an overlap between the sections.

Section 2(1)(*a*)
A person is guilty of an offence if he by deception dishonestly ". . . secures the remission of the whole or part of any existing liability to make a payment, whether his own liability or another's."

Mens rea. The *mens rea* required is dishonesty (see above). There is no requirement of an intention to make permanent deprivation.

Actus reus. The words "secures the remission" indicate that the legal obligation to make payment must be extinguished, and therefore although permanent deprivation is not specifically mentioned, it is implied. It is not completely clear what the difference is between remitting liability and foregoing payment, which is the wording used in section 2(1)(*b*).

The liability remitted does not have to be the liability of the defendant.

It may be that of a third party on whose behalf D operates the deception. The liability may be remitted wholly or only in part.

The provision refers to an existing liability. It may have only existed for a few moments, as where a contract is formed at the checkout, and deception then used as to payment, but the liability must have been incurred before it is avoided. Section 2(1)(c) covers the situation where the liability does not already exist. (See below.)

Section 2(1)(b)

Under this section it is an offence if a person by deception:

> "with intent to make permanent default in whole or in part on any existing liability to make a payment, or with intent to let another do so, dishonestly induces the creditor or any person claiming payment on behalf of the creditor to wait for payment . . . or to forego payment."

Mens rea. Dishonesty is required (see above). There must also be an intent to make permanent default. This is therefore a crime of specific intent. This may be one way of deciding which offence has been committed in case which seem to overlap with other prohibitions.

Actus reus. The creditor or his representative must be induced to forego payment either willingly or because he feels he has no choice. This element of inducement is another factor distinguishing this provision from the last. In section 2(1)(a) the creditor may not even know that the debt has been remitted. The deception may have led him to believe that he has been paid. In section 2(1)(b) the deception induces the creditor to make the offer to the defendant, although it may be only because he feels he has no alternative.

As mentioned above it is not entirely clear what is meant by foregoing payment and how it differs from remitting liability but the most likely explanation is that foregoing payment does not extinguish the debt. Under the law of contract the fact that the creditor agrees to forego payment or accepts a lesser sum in payment does not end the contract and relieve the debtor of liability unless there is a new contract wth fresh consideration. In cases where payment is foregone therefore the creditor still has a civil law claim to it.

The liability referred to in the section can only be the liability of the person evading it.

Authority: *Attewell-Hughes* (1991). D had opened accounts in the name of others and had run up overdrafts. The liability he was evading was in fact legally the liability of others. The Court held that section 2(1)(b) only referred to D's own liability, and did not cover this situation. The only alternative basis for a charge was enabling another to evade that other's liability, and that was not appropriate here either.

Section 2(3). This subsection states that a person who is induced to take a cheque or other security in payment of a pre-existing liability is to be treated not as having been paid, but as having been induced to wait for payment. A person who writes a cheque, or uses a credit card, knowing that he is exceeding his authority, will be liable under section 2(1)(*b*), because the creditor is induced to wait for payment. Dishonesty will still need to be proved, and there must be an intent to make *permanent* default.

Section 2(1)(*c*)

Under this provision an offence is committed if a person by deception "dishonestly obtains any exemption from or abatement of liability to make a payment."

Actus reus. The wording of the provision covers both the situation where liability is reduced (abatement), or avoided altogether (exemption). Section 2(4) states that obtaining includes obtaining for another or enabling another to obtain.

No pre-existing liability is required under this provision. It therefore covers the situation where the deception operates before or at the time liability is incurred, to prevent all or some part of it arising, as in the situation where someone claims to be over 65 to gain reduced rates of entry to the cinema. There the deception operates and liability is abated before the debt is incurred.

Authority: *Sibartie* (1983). D had bought a season ticket for the first and last part of his journey on the Underground, and travelled the middle part without paying. At an intercharge station he flashed a ticket at the inspector hoping to avoid detection. He was charged with attempting the offence under section 2(1)(*c*).

On appeal the court held that the wording of section 2(1)(*c*) must be given its ordinary natural meaning. A jury could have found that what D did was an attempt to obtain exemption from liability to make payment. The conviction was affirmed. The fact that the facts might also indicate an offence under section 2(1)(*b*) was irrelevant, as there was a certain amount of overlap between the two provisions.

This case indicates the uncertainty of the dividing lines between the different offences under section 2(1). There is also an overlap (see above) between section 2(1)(*a*) and 2(1)(*b*).

MAKING OFF WITHOUT PAYMENT

Under section 3(1) of the 1978 Act, if a person knows that payment on the spot is required or expected for goods or services, he commits an offence if he dishonestly makes off without paying, intending not to pay.

Mens rea

Knowledge. The defendant must know that payment on the spot is required or expected.

Intent to avoid payment. This is a crime of specific intent. There is no requirement of intention to permanently avoid payment in the section, but the courts have read this requirement in.

Authority: *Allen* (1984). D was not liable for an offence under section 3 because the prosecution had not proved an intent *never* to pay.

Actus reus

Making off. This means leaving the actual point where payment is due, such as going past the till and into the lobby. It is not always easy to decide when the offence has actually been committed.

Authority: *Brooks and Brooks* (1983). Ds were father and daughter who had a meal in a restaurant with a third person and attempted to leave without paying. The father had passed the spot where payment should have been made but was still on the premises, near the back door. His conviction was affirmed on appeal. The daughter's was quashed because she had a possible defence on which the jury were not directed.

Without having paid. Section 2(3) does not apply to section 3 and it is therefore assumed that the person paying with a dud cheque has "paid" for the purposes of section 3.

Section 3 does not cover the situation where the debt is not legally enforceable (section 3(3)).

Authority: *Troughton* v. *Metropolitan Police* (1987). D was a drunk passenger in a taxi, who did not tell the driver his address. The driver stopped at a police station to try and sort the matter out, and D ran off. He was charged with making off without payment, but the court held that there was no liability. The taxi driver was in breach of contract for taking him somewhere other than his destination, and there was therefore no legal obligation on D to pay at the time he made off.

Finally, and most importantly, there is *no* requirement of deception for liability under section 3. It is designed to cover the *D.P.P.* v. *Ray* situation (see above), where a strained interpretation of the concept of deception was necessary in order to convict the defendant.

SUMMARY

The main topics for revision are:

Common elements in deception offences

Deception (*Feeny*)
Words or Conduct (*Charles, Gilmartin*)
Deception by Omission (*Firth*), Fact, Law or Present Intentions
Cause of Obtaining (*Charles, Lambie, Laverty*)
Dishonesty (*Ghosh, Woolven, Price*)

Obtaining property by deception

Actus Reus
Property, Obtaining, Belonging to Another
Mens Rea
Intention to Permanently Deprive
Overlap Between Theft and Deception

Obtaining a pecuniary advantage by deception

Section 16(2)(*b*)
Section 16(2)(*c*) (*Callender*)

Obtaining services by deception

Section 1, Theft Act 1978
Actus Reus, Obtaining Services

Evasion of liability by deception

Section 2(1)(*a*), *Mens Rea, Actus Reus*
Section 2(1)(*b*), *Mens Rea, Actus Reus*, (*Attewell-Hughes*), section 2(3)
Section 2(1)(*c*), *Mens Rea, Actus Reus* (*Sibartie*)

Making off without payment

Mens Rea
Dishonesty, Intent to Avoid Payment (*Allen*)
Actus Reus
Making Off (*Brooks and Brooks*)
Without having Paid (*Troughton* v. *Met. Police*)
No Deception

11. SAMPLE EXAMINATION QUESTIONS

This chapter sets out some problem questions as examples of how certain issues might be presented in an examination. Basic plans of suggested answers are also provided.

For revision purposes the student should first attempt these questions, at a stage when he thinks his revision is complete, without consulting the answer plans. He can then compare his answers with the plans and genuinely gauge the progress of his revision and the extent of his understanding. This process will also enable him to pinpoint particular areas or topics he has misunderstood or not fully grasped. Extra revision time can then be spent on those topics.

The answering of questions in examination conditions, particularly problem questions, is a skill which can improve considerably with practice. The added advantage of consolidating revision in this way is that the student's examination technique will improve as his knowledge does, and this, too, can help to achieve a good grade.

SOME GENERAL GUIDELINES

Some general points should be borne in mind by the student in any examination, whatever the subject:

The question paper

Read the question paper through carefully and completely before making a choice of questions. Although questions are not deliberately designed to mislead and confuse, students can often misunderstand a question on first reading and either mistakenly decide they are unable to answer it, or answer it in the wrong way. Time spent in careful reading and calculation as to which questions the student can best answer is time well spent. First reactions are not always the best ones and a re-reading can often indicate another question which is easier than first thought, or an initial choice which has extra complications. It is better to spend the time at the beginning of the examination finding this out than to discover it when you are half way through a question and have wasted precious time.

Timing

Timing in an examination is crucial. It is the downfall of many a student who finds he has only time to write two or three lines on the last question and therefore cannot do it, or himself, justice.

It is essential that the student keeps an eye on the time throughout the examination and devotes a minimum time to each question. Obviously there will be some questions he can answer better than others and he will take longer answering these, but it is important to remember that the first 10 or so marks of any question are easier to achieve, and are given for more basic information, than the last 10–15. A student is therefore more likely to gain extra marks by devoting the last 15 minutes to tackling the next question than he is by continuing with the present.

The plan

All written answers, even, or especially, in examination conditions, should start with a plan so that the student can see the beginning, middle and end of his answer before he starts in detail. The plan concentates the mind on the whole of the question, helps the student to omit irrelevant information and to answer the question more logically, and it gives him confidence. A plan can make time rather than waste time and if the answer is not finished it gives the examiner an indication that the student has thought through the whole question. Never dispense with a plan.

Layout

Every answer should have an introduction, where the student outlines the main points, and a conclusion where he summarises them and states his opinions if relevant. This does not necessarily lead to undue repetition, but provides the examiner with a clear, well laid out answer that is easy to follow. Both student and examiner can easily see whether any main points have been omitted and whether the process of argument is logically followed through.

Relevance

One of the commonest mistakes made by the students in examination questions is failing to answer the question asked. Relevance is of the utmost importance. Marks will not be given for irrelevant material, however accurate or illuminating, and valuable time is wasted in providing it. If the question says advise A, then the student should *not* advise B. An examiner is primarily interested in the student's ability to *apply* the law in the particular manner asked, and not in his ability to write all he knows about subject X. He should be selective, leave irrelevant material out, even if he has spent hours learning it, and simply answer the question asked.

Problem-solving

The answering of problem-type questions or "case studies" seems to present particular difficulties for students, and demands a special technique of its own.

The basic requirement is to apply the law to the given fact situation, working only on the facts given and not any assumed facts. *All* the different possibilities must be considered before the student gives his own opinion as to the most likely conclusion, with reasons.

The secret of a successful technique in answering problem questions is to integrate the factual analysis with the relevant legal authorities, giving as much factual and legal detail as is necessary without turning the answer into little more than a series of case notes. Depending on the importance and relevance of the case, detail required may vary from the name of the case only to a critical discussion of the opinions of various judges. The skill in deciding this is something which a student must develop for himself by trial and error, as it varies from case to case and question to question. The more practice a student has, the more skilled he becomes.

Procedure in problem-solving

The student should follow this, or a similar procedure when answering problem questions:

Make a plan noting the important factual occurrences, the relevant areas of law, and any important cases or statutes.

Work through the facts according to each "mini" situation, normally in chronological order. Re-state the facts and state the law which applies, citing any relevant case or statute to the degree necessary to make the point you wish.

Give a conclusion in each "mini" situation, *but* leave all options open and consider all alternatives.

Move on to the next "mini" situation and repeat the procedure, remembering if necessary to refer back to previous linking facts. Once a legal principle, or case or statute has been fully explained then any further references to it can be brief. There is no need to be repetitive; the important skill is *applying* the law to the facts and not merely stating the principles.

Summarise, drawing all the "mini" situations together. Re-state briefly all the possibilities you have considered, and the possible alternatives, citing the main authorities again, by name only.

Finally give your own opinion and conclusion in the terms asked for by the question (*e.g.* "advise X," "consider the legal issues," "what defences are available to Y," etc.). Give only the answer asked for and no more, but give your reasons for your conclusions. Make sure that your opinions are legally tenable and supported by your discussion of the issues.

QUESTIONS

(1) Bernadette volunteers to go along on Deirdre's school outing as extra adult supervision is needed. She is in charge of a small group of girls. At the seaside she sunbathes while they paddle. On hearing a scream she sits up to see two girls, Elizabeth and Jane, out of their depth and drowning. She mistakenly assumes that they are playing and that there is no risk. William, a passer-by dives in and rescues the girls. Over-reacting, he

gives Elizabeth unnecessary mouth to mouth ressucitation and heart massage. Unknown to him, she has a weak heart, has heart failure and she dies. While all this is going on Jane is ignored and is not seen by Bernadette for several hours. She catches pneumonia due to her exposure, is ill for several months and then dies.

Discuss the criminal liability, if any, of Bernadette and William.

(2) Angus shows Charles how to pick a lock. He does not know exactly what Charles intends to do, although he knows he is going to "sort out" his boss, who owes him money.

Charles breaks into his boss's house and steals a painting which he estimates is of the same value as the money he is owed. He is charged with burglary, and Angus is charged as a secondary party. Charles' defence is that he thought he had a right to do what he did, as he saw it as the only way of getting what he was owed. Angus's defence is that he did not know exactly what Charles would do but he thought he would simply try and get his money back.

Advise Angus and Charles as to their criminal liability and the availability of any defences.

(3) Angus and Charles go out for a drink. Angus, knowing Charles is a diabetic who carefully controls his drinking, spikes Charles' orange juice with vodkas. Charles, having had nothing to eat, becomes drunk very quickly and suffers a hypoglycaemic episode. During this episode he attacks and seriously injures another customer. Angus, realising that the spiked drink was the start of all the trouble, is too frightened to interfere, so hides and does nothing. Discuss the criminal liability of Charles and Angus.

(4) Charles finds a valuable ring on the floor of Angus's living room during a party. He puts it in his pocket, intending to find out who it belongs to, but forgets about it.

He hears the next day that the ring belongs to Bernadette, and he tells her he has it, offering to return it to her. She asks him to look after it for her while she is on holiday. Being short of money he pawns it, honestly believing that he will be able to redeem it before she returns from holiday.

Meanwhile Angus, who still thinks the ring is lost, is in a panic. Charles offers to find an identical replacement ring for him if he will pay him a fee of £50 in advance. Angus agrees, and writes him a cheque backed by a cheque card, even though he knows this will create an overdraft for which he does not have permission.

Discuss the possible liabilities of Angus and Charles under the Theft Acts.

(5) Charles, while drunk, breaks into a shed in someone's garden to

sleep there one night. He mistakenly believes the garden belongs to a friend of his. Ursula, who is sleeping in the house, hears a noise and comes out to investigate. When she enters the shed Charles grabs her, forces her to the floor and has intercourse with her. He then pulls off rings and a bracelet she is wearing, holding her down to prevent her struggling. Afterwards he claims that because of his drunken state he mistook Ursula for his wife.

Advise Charles as to his criminal liability.

(6) Angus agrees to buy Charles's lawnmower. He writes a cheque backed by a cheque card, although he has had a letter from his bank asking him to return the card until his overdraft is paid off. Charles asked him to wait until the cheque is cleared before he takes the lawnmower away. The next day Angus sees the lawnmower in Charles' garden and, as he feels it is already his, decides to take it.

Discuss Angus's liability for theft and/or deception offences.

---

12. ANSWER PLANS

The following are plans of answers to the questions set out in Chapter 11. They are rather fuller than a plan a student might make in an examination situation, but they give a general indication of how such plans might be made. They do not attempt to give a "right" answer. There rarely is one "right" answer, and any conclusion the student reaches must be his own. Provided that the relevant legal authorities are cited and the student can use them to support his conclusion, it should make no difference that the examiner disagrees with him.

QUESTION 1

Legal issues
Liability for Omissions, Unlawful Act Manslaughter, Manslaughter by Gross Negligence, Causation.

Summary

Bernadette
Bernadette has voluntarily undertaken responsibility so may be liable for omitting to act. *Stone and Dobinson.*

Elizabeth's death. She omits to act when she should. Was she grossly negligent? Was death or serious injury foreseeable? What would a reasonable person have done? *Kong Chuek Kwan* criteria. Is this a "loophole" case? *Reid.*

Was B's omission a substantial cause of death or was W's action an intervening act which breaks the chain? *Malcherek.* Was her omission still a substantial cause despite the new act? Is victim's weak heart relevant? *Blaue.*

Does W's treatment constitute negligent medical treatment, and if so, does it make a difference? *Cheshire.*

Jane's death. Omission to care for girl. (See above.)

Gross negligence, reasonable standard, foresight of slight/serious harm. (See above.)

Causation, operating and substantial cause of death. (See above.)

William

William's act has caused Elizabeth's death. Has he committed an unlawful act? An assault? Offences Against the Person Act 1861. *Savage.* Would the reasonable man realise the risk of some injury, however slight? *Church.* William did not know of the weak heart. Would the reasonable man have known? *Dawson.* Is William's act a cause of death? *Watson, Armstrong.*

Was William grossly negligent? (See above.)

QUESTION 2

Legal issues

Parties to Crime. *Mens Rea* of Secondary Parties. Burglary. Claim of Right in Theft.

Summary

Parties to crime, aiding and abetting, *A.G.'s Ref. No. 1 of 1975.*

Mens rea of secondary parties, knowledge required. Does Angus have sufficient knowledge? How much detail does he need to know? *Bainbridge, Maxwell.* Did he *know* that Charles would do something illegal? Is his defence relevant if a jury believe him?

Charles: has he committed a burglary? Section 9, Theft Act 1968. Section 9(1)(*a*) requires entry as a trespasser *with intent* to commit theft. Did he so intend? This is a crime of specific intent—necessary *mens rea*?

Charles' defence of claim of right. Section 2 of 1968 Act, definition of when a defendant is *not* dishonest. Does it apply here? Test is subjective, but he must believe he had a right in law, not just a moral right.

If Charles is not liable, is there an offence committed at all? Can Angus be liable as a secondary party? *Thornton* v. *Mitchell.*

QUESTION 3

Legal issues

Defences. Automatism. Intoxication. Assault. Sections 18, 20, Offences Against the Person Act 1861. Participation in Crime. Procuring. Liability for Omissions.

Summary

Charles

Assault under section 20, 1861 Act. Grievous bodily harm, *Wilson*, crime of basic intent, *Grimshaw*.

Assault under section 18, crime of specific intent, *Belfon*. Can Charles have this specific intent in these circumstances?

Defences. Intoxication and its effect on liability for crimes of basic intent, different rules for crimes of specific intent, *Majewski*. Involuntary intoxication; does it make a difference? Is he reckless? Possible argument based on *Hardie* would help Charles here.

Alternative defence of automatism, *Quick*, *Bailey*. Is it relevant that the drink is taken involuntarily and therefore automatism is not self-induced? Is *mens rea* negatived? Is there an internal or external cause here? *Hennessey*.

Angus

Is he liable as a secondary party for procuring? *A.G.'s Ref. No. 1 of 1975*. *Mens Rea* for secondary parties, *Blakely*. If Angus is a secondary party, relevance to his liability of Charles' defence? *Bourne*.

Should Angus have stepped in and prevented the violence? Is he under a duty to act due to his own prior conduct? *Miller*. What could he be liable for?

QUESTION 4

Legal issues

Theft Act 1968. Appropriation. Intention Permanently to Deprive. Dishonesty. Obtaining property by deception, section 15, 1968 Act. Obtaining a pecuniary advantage by deception, section 16, 1968 Act. Evasion of liability by deception, section 2, 1978 Act.

Summary

Charles

Charles finds the ring, *i.e.* comes by it lawfully, therefore not theft. Appropriation, section 3, 1968 Act. A later assumption of the rights of an owner can be appropriation. When is the moment of appropriation,

Gomez. Assumption of some rights of an owner will be sufficient, *Morris*. Pawning is an appropriation of some rights.

Intent permanently to deprive, section 6(2), 1968 Act. Parting with property under a condition he may not be able to fulfil is *deemed* an intent permanently to deprive. This covers the pawning situation. Irrelevant that he intends to redeem it and return it.

Dishonesty, section 2 of 1968 Act, partial definition, this situation not covered. *Ghosh* applies, two stage test; is D dishonest by reasonable standards, and did he realise that he was? Applied here, is Charles dishonest when he honestly thought he could redeem and return it and intended to do so? What might a jury decide?

Has Charles obtained £50 from Angus by deception? What is the deception? Is he obliged to tell Angus of the whereabouts of the ring? *D.P.P.* v. *Ray*. Implied deception? By omission? *Callender*. Does a deception cause the obtaining? *Laverty*.

Is there an overlap with theft? *Gomez*.

Angus

Does Angus obtain a pecuniary advantage by deception? Section 16(2)(*b*). From whom? What is the deception? *Charles*. On whom does it operate? Does this matter?

Does Angus evade his liability by deception under section 2 of the 1978 Act? Does he induce his creditor to wait for payment? Section 2(3). Does he intend permanently to default on the debt?

QUESTION 5

Legal issues

Burglary. Robbery. Sections 9 and 8 of Theft Act 1968. Rape. Intoxication. Mistake.

Summary

Burglary, section 9, 1968 Act. Entering a building as a trespasser, is Charles a trespasser? What constitutes a building or part of a building? Are sheds, outhouses, etc., covered?

Section 9(1)(*a*), entry with intent, an offence of specific intent, covers intent to commit rape, theft, g.b.h. or criminal damage. Did Charles enter with such intent? Relevance of intoxication? *Majewski*. If not, is there an offence under section 9(1)(*b*), having entered as a trespasser and then actually committing theft or g.b.h.? Relevance of his mistake about owner? Relevance of intoxication? Is this kind of burglary a crime of basic or specific intent?

Does Charles commit theft? Appropriation of Ursula's jewellery?

Does he commit g.b.h.; holding Ursula down will not constitute really serious injury, *Saunders*, but will the rape? Is it rape? Relevance of mistake,

R. Relevance of intoxication again. Basic or specific intent? *Majewski.*

Does he commit robbery as well as burglary; use of force before or at time of stealing and in order to steal, section 8, 1968 Act?

QUESTION 6

Legal issues

Evasion of Liability by Deception. Theft Act 1978.

Summary

Angus agrees to buy the lawnmower, and his liability arises then.

Section 2(1)(*b*), 1987 Act, does he induce creditor to wait for payment?

Section 2(3) covers writing cheques as inducing creditor to wait.

Is he dishonest? Same meaning as for theft, *Ghosh* applies, subjective, two stage test.

Does he intend to make permanent default?

What is the deception? Conduct, giving cheque and card, *Charles, Lambie*, implied representation of right to use the card.

Angus takes the lawnmower the next day. Appropriation, section 3 of 1968 Act, assumption of owner's rights. *Morris, Gomez.*

Belonging to another, ownership, possession or control.

To whom does the property belong? Can Angus steal his own property? *Turner.*

Dishonesty, section 2, 1968 Act, claim of right. Is Angus dishonest?

INDEX